I0436770

Alcohol and Ethics

The Myths and Facts

by
James McDonough

authorHOUSE™

1663 LIBERTY DRIVE, SUITE 200
BLOOMINGTON, INDIANA 47403
(800) 839-8640
WWW.AUTHORHOUSE.COM

© 2005 James McDonough. All Rights Reserved.

No part of this book may be reproduced, stored in a retrieval system, or transmitted by any means without the written permission of the author.

First published by AuthorHouse 07/21/05

ISBN: 1-4208-6853-5 (sc)

Printed in the United States of America
Bloomington, Indiana

This book is printed on acid-free paper.

To My Wife and Daughters

whose Love and Support Saved My Life

Table of Contents

I My Story 1

II What I've Learned About Alcoholism 20

III Common Misperceptions About Alcoholism.............42

IV. What's Wrong with Common Misperceptions About
Alcoholism..56

V. Correct Perceptions About Alcoholism 66

VI Implications for the Future 82

VII What To Do If You Think You Have the Disease of
Alcoholism...107

VIII What To Do If Someone You Know Has This Disease.......135

IX Conclusion 149

I
My Story

What It Was Like-My Normal Life

The summary of my life sounds relatively normal when compared to the lives of the men and women who grew up and entered adulthood around same time that I did. I managed an above average academic record in elementary and secondary schools, went to college, where I initially performed poorly, and later improved to above average. I took a liking to the idea of teaching at the college level as a goal for my life's work and because of the Viet Nam War, I faced the draft after graduation, so I took the full four year course load of ROTC, determined to go into the military as a Commissioned Officer, if I had to serve one way or the other. I graduated, obtained my commission as a Second Lieutenant in the Army with a delay of entry into Active Service to attend graduate school and set out to earn my Master of Arts degree. I worked full-time during the summer vacations and part-time during the school years. While in graduate school, I worked both full-time and part-time jobs. None of these jobs would attract attention, but they allowed me spending money and helped pay tuition and fees.

Late in my senior year of college, I met and fell in love with the woman I would marry and began a two year courtship that culminated in our marriage, immediately following our respective graduations and preceding, by a few months, my entry into the Army. We traveled with my various duty assignments over the next years, never staying more than four years at a time in any one place. We had two daughters, who won my heart entirely from their births and still have it today. Over the years, though I often lacked the capacity to adequately express it, my love for my wife and daughters grew progressively and it continues to do so. Our family life went normally, at least for a while, and our daughters did the kinds of things that most girls do during their formative years.

While moving every couple years began to take its toll on us, we experienced the same types of challenges that many military families experience. I retired after twenty five years of service and started a second career that I continue to pursue now. Our daughters have either completed their higher educations or continue to pursue it. My wife teaches elementary school and has done that for the past 15 years. We own a lovely home; one that I never would have dreamed of owning in my younger years. In a nutshell, my life and my family's lives appear nearly perfect, but in reality, a much different story more accurately captures our life stories, because I am an alcoholic and that disease nearly killed me and nearly destroyed everything worth having in life for my family.

I do not exaggerate when I write these sentences. I intend that people who suffer from the disease of alcoholism, and it is a disease, as well as their family members, who suffer terribly, too, will learn something from my experiences. If I can help someone else recover and/or avoid the damage I did to myself and my family, I will have succeeded in accomplishing something with this book. I also intend to demonstrate that the myriad of myths about alcoholism that abound within our society do not hold up in light of logical and scientific analysis into the alcoholic condition. As a result, the types of moral and legal judgments that many people make about alcoholic people do not make sense. We should change laws and approaches to the whole problem of alcohol addiction. I hope to show how this might work.

I do not want to diminish the amount of suffering that practicing alcoholics usually inflict on their families and close friends. We alcoholics do tremendous emotional and psychological (and sometimes physical) damage to those whose lives intimately touch ours. But, to understand alcoholism as a disease and the alcoholic as a sick person, who for the most part does not intend to hurt others and, in many cases, is unaware that these injuries occur, may help everyone involved. We can all move toward recovery from the nightmare that alcoholism generates and a wonderful life free of alcohol's ravages. Here's what I have learned about this complicated disease and recovery from it.

James McDonough

What It Was Like—The True Story

I started to drink alcohol at age 18 during the summer between my senior year in high school and freshman year in college. I had previous knowledge of alcoholic drinking, because my father drank for the first nine or ten years of my life and I accompanied him to various bars in our neighborhood during some of his excursions. His brothers and sisters drank too, so that I saw first-hand how alcohol can affect people during several family reunions that we attended. One of my uncles lost a few jobs and went into in-patient treatment at a time when I could remember these events. But even with this background, I liked what alcohol did for me when I became familiar with it for the first time. In retrospect, I know now that I never drank "normally" or socially. I drank only because it made me feel good and I craved that feeling. But at the beginning of my drinking career, I did not exhibit any abnormal character or behavioral traits. For years, most people thought of me as a social drinker and I thought that of myself, as well. I had the ability to "hold my liquor." At the time, I thought that a sign of masculinity, but I now know that it signified a growing tolerance for alcohol that further indicates alcoholism in an early stage.

Through college and graduate school, I drank on some weekends, usually at social events and nearly every day during the summers when I did not have to study. Sometimes, but not often, I'd get drunk, by my definition of "drunk," which is much different from the medical and legal definitions of "drunk."." I consumed less volume than many of the guys with whom I played football and basketball when in school. Still, I loved the feeling of serenity that drinking alcohol seemed to always produce. I drank myself sick for the first time at age 23, decided to quit during the hangover that spree created, and then drank again the next weekend when I felt back to normal. I had my first blackout at age 27 and resolved to not drink again during my recovery from that bout, but started drinking the next weekend when I felt better. Soon, because I mistakenly believed that I could control whether or not I developed a drinking problem, I made rules for when and how much I would drink. I would only drink two beers and two shots of hard liquor every other night. Thus controlling my drinking, I thought, would ensure that I would not become an alcoholic. Now I know that by making rules for when and how much I drank, I demonstrated a classic symptom of alcoholism. People who do not have drinking problems do not make rules about when, where and how much they drink. They do not even think about drinking.

At various times in my military career, a move or a job change would create stress and I would change my drinking rules accordingly, sometimes disregarding the rules altogether. By the time I reached age 30, I drank some alcohol nearly every day. Though I realized that my consumption rate had increased, I managed to trivialize and rationalize this change easily. As my career blossomed, I deluded myself into believing that I could not be alcoholic and succeed to the degree I was succeeding, confirming for myself that I did not have a problem with drinking alcohol. I did not realize that though my career did not suffer yet, my family had already begun to feel the affects of my drinking. Most alcoholics I know have similar stories. The families always seem to suffer first and most.

At one point, my wife mentioned to me that my drinking affected our relationship and I promised her that I would quit. I meant that promise when I spoke it, but the next day, I drank again, rationalizing that I would quit the following day. I continued waiting for the next day to quit drinking for the next ten years. Though I don't recall my wife speaking to me about my drinking again for quite a while after that incident, I now know she watched me closely and formulated the opinion that I had chosen alcohol over her. Our relationship began a gradual degradation that would lead to complete breakup about nine years later.

I began drinking greater amounts of alcohol on a daily basis without consciously thinking about it. Though I falsely believed that because I did not drink in the mornings or early afternoons, I did not have a drinking problem, I sometimes thought that I could improve my life by quitting drinking. But, such thoughts got rationalized away with the delusion that tomorrow presented a better opportunity to quit drinking. The types of assignments I drew in the Army during this period allowed me to drink heavily without professional repercussion. I worked hard on my physical conditioning and as that improved, so did my delusion that I still controlled my alcohol intake. In fact, that continued to increase gradually over the period of years, even as my aerobic and strength conditioning improved.

My wife spoke to me on more occasions about how much I drank as these years progressed and I decided that I could deceive her about how much I drank by not drinking in front of her. So, without considering the potential consequences of my actions, I started sneaking drinks in an attempt to keep my marriage intact and still get my fill of alcohol. Though I managed to excel in my career, my candle burned at both ends. After more remonstrating from my wife, I decided to make a change in my behavior; I switched to drinking vodka in the belief that other people could not smell it on my breath. This tactic seemed to work for a period of time, but as the amount of vodka I consumed increased steadily, I could not entirely hide this consumption from others.

About 20 years into my drinking career, I discovered that taking a drink or two in the mornings on days when I did not have to work produced a great feeling and for a short period of time, this newly established practice worked well for me. During all of this time, I could not see how much alcohol had consumed my life. I started carrying alcohol in my cars, in case I would find myself somewhere where I could not readily and legally get it. I sometimes avoided doing things or attending social functions that I used to enjoy, because I could not drink alcohol there. My personal relationships suffered, but I became oblivious to all of that. I also developed moderate to severe physical symptoms on the occasions when I could not drink, like sweating, shaking and anxiety.

Finally, my wife had had enough of this and asked me for a divorce. This action surprised me, as I had become so delusional that I didn't see any reason in my behavior that would justify her wanting a divorce. I blamed her for the consequences that followed the divorce. But, through this stage of my life, I continued to drink heavily and soon the symptoms became too much for me to hide from my superiors, so I sought professional treatment. Though I successfully completed this program, I didn't apply what I learned there to my own case and began drinking again once they officially severed me from their observation.

For several years, I tried to prove to myself that I did not have a problem with alcohol. I reduced the amounts I drank on a daily basis and consciously avoided drinking on occasions when someone in authority, who may have known about my history of out-patient treatment, might see me drink. But, all of the pressure I felt to conceal my drinking and struggles to keep the amount I drank down, did not indicate to me that I was an alcoholic. Any sane person who knew how much effort I expended in these endeavors every day would immediately conclude that I was alcoholic and needed help. I went through periods of voluntary dryness and involuntary dryness (my duties precluded me from drinking), but I always found a time when I could start drinking again and I always took the opportunity. I discovered that long periods of abstinence from alcohol did not permit me to begin drinking "normally" again. Within a short time of starting drinking again, I consumed as much, or more, than I had when I stopped drinking weeks, months or even a year before.

I voluntarily went back into a treatment program again, but my real motivation came from fear of discovery and professional ruin. My ex-wife and I re-married and took up life together again with our daughters, but I still had the craving to drink and began experimenting with sneaking it again. I volunteered to attend an in-patient treatment program, but failed to follow the professionals' advice on leaving the treatment facility and got drunk a few weeks after I left. I retired from the military and started another career, but kept drinking. All of the details of this period of my life become confusing, but to summarize them, all of the problems that most of us associate with alcoholism came my way: lost family relationships, lost jobs, arrests, legal issues, health problems, the works. By the 33rd year of my drinking career, I had "hit bottom." I found myself without a home, without a job, without a friend, with little money, unable to eat without becoming ill, and without hope. The momentary euphoria that alcohol sometimes gave me became my only spark in life. I had moved into the terrible cycle of fear, guilt, remorse, and self-pity that resulted in one drinking bout after another, characterized by periods of blackouts, unconsciousness and irrational behavior. I feared drinking and not drinking at the same time. I had become totally hopeless.

What Happened

Through my wife's efforts and those of counselors who had tried to help me in the past, I managed to get into another in-patient treatment program. In the early days of that program, I felt a hopelessness that I could never have imagined possible earlier in my life. I had the conscious thought that I would prefer death to the way I felt then. In the words of the authors of the book, *Alcoholics Anonymous,* "I stood at the turning point."[1] Though in a position that clearly had only one rational option for action, I continued under the control of alcohol enough that I could not see my only option. The change in my life happened when my counselor told me what I had to do in a way that drove home the seriousness of my condition. I would die within a year if I kept on the way I had lived. He would not waste any more time on me, if I did not do what he told me to do and I would end up on the street, probably to die homeless, friendless, hopeless. I decided to try his suggestions for getting better.

My counselor told me to change my attitude; I should become grateful for what I had rather than bitter for what I did not have. After all, the problems of my life resulted from my own actions. Though I balked at the idea that I had anything for which to be grateful, my counselor pointed out that I had a disease that afflicted many people and many of them did not wake up that morning, so I had that for which to thank God or someone other than me. I ate three daily meals at the treatment facility, another blessing for which I should thank someone, since many other alcoholics did not have that luxury. I had four walls and a roof around me and many alcoholics did not have that. I had counselors and other patients who cared about me and many alcoholics did not have that benefit. He had given me a starting point that I had not considered before. From that, I made up two lists, one of the things for which I should be grateful and one of the things for which I should not have gratitude. The first list ran considerably longer than the second. I had begun to turn the corner.

I started praying every morning when I woke up and every evening before I fell asleep, something I hadn't considered doing, let alone done, for many years. I openly spoke to the members of my therapy group every day about how I felt about everything that had happened in my life and about the future. I learned to identify feelings, emotions that I had almost totally obliterated through drinking alcohol for years. I needed the help of the chart the counselors provided that listed the many feelings that humans experience to determine what I felt. I wrote letters to my parents, both of whom had passed away years ago, telling them how I felt, and I read the letters aloud to my therapy group. I wrote letters to my daughters, telling them how I felt, that I read to my therapy group. I wrote a letter to my wife, telling her how I felt about her that I read to my therapy group. My wife wrote a letter to me, telling me how she felt, that I read to my therapy group. Demons that I had suppressed inside me, strong, negative feelings, came out. I learned to cry and not be ashamed. I discovered new feelings: freedom from guilt, serenity, sobriety.

As part of the in-patient treatment program, we attended nightly meetings of Alcoholics Anonymous or Narcotics Anonymous. Though I had attended such meetings when I participated in the out-patient programs in the past, I now listened to the discussions and paid attention, as if I belonged there. Previously, I had rejected the idea that I belonged there; those people were alcoholics and addicts. Now I knew I belonged there; I fit in perfectly and they welcomed me unconditionally. I read the book, *Alcoholics Anonymous*, and recorded my feelings about it in my daily journal, which I submitted to my counselor for review every day. I read other books and attended educational classes about my disease every afternoon. For the first time in as long as I could remember, I felt enthusiasm for life. I wanted to live. A huge burden of guilt, self-pity and fear had left me. I realized that even as poor as I had become monetarily, I was richer in another way than I had been, probably forever. I knew myself and began to like me.

After 28 days in the program, I left the center to resume my life. This time, I had the curious feeling that I would not drink again. I had begun to recover from a terrible illness. This time, unlike my experience of two years before that, I did what my counselors told me to do and I did not do what they told me not to do. I started going to AA meetings every other day or so. I went to the after care group meetings once a week for people like me, most of whom wanted to rebuild their lives. I wrote in my journal; I found other things to do with my time, like reading, exercising and meditating/praying, all of which were free. I found a place to live and started looking for a job. I felt once again like a contributing member of society and to my family. Gradually, I lost the last vestiges of the symptoms of withdrawal from alcohol. I felt healthy again.

I decided to read the 12 steps of the AA recovery program often and try to live my life in accordance with them. I found that I had never understood the first step and that failing in that important piece of the process, I had no chance to recover. I decided that I had to translate the wording from Step 1 into something that meant action on my part. So, I adopted as my translation of Step 1, words I had heard in a number of AA meetings: I can never drink safely again. By using this realization as the foundation of my individual recovery program, I avoided the pitfall of making a promise that I had made and broken numerous times before, i.e. that I will never drink alcohol again. By simply realizing that I cannot drink safely ever again, I formulated a plan of action and an intention to carry it out. The plan simply requires me to arrange my life in such a way that I don't drink alcohol today or one day at a time. If necessary, I can break days down into hours, hours into minutes, minutes into seconds.

For me, drinking had occupied so much of my time that I had to figure out how to spend the time I used to spend drinking. Praying, meditating, reading, exercising, rebuilding personal relationships and resting used up most of the time I used to spend getting drunk. I concentrated on the several phrases that AA has adopted to help those of us in recovery to deal with life without using alcohol. "Easy does it." I work on taking my time, not expecting immediate gratification for every whim I have, not rashly acting on impulse, thinking my actions through before acting. I have experienced much less anxiety since I've adopted this phrase into my philosophy of life. I have stopped competing against everyone and everything. I only try to do the best that I can do, without regard to how that performance measures up against others or some standards. I no longer obsess that someone else will creep past me in the game of life; instead, I play the course, not the other players. I learned that I imposed on myself much of the stress I felt in life during my drinking days, which I used as an excuse to drink. I placed that stress on myself with unreasonable expectations of what I should and could accomplish.

"But for the grace of God," another of the AA slogans by which I try to live my life has helped me substantially, too. As I became more aware of my surroundings and the events going on in the world, I saw that many alcoholic people ended up in prison for actions they perpetrated while under the influence, many of which they probably do not remember because they occurred in alcohol induced blackouts. I saw a number of newcomers to AA meetings, obviously still deeply in denial about their diseases, much like I had been ten years before. I saw extended family members who clearly suffer from alcoholism, but continue to drink and destroy their lives. I heard of former patients with whom I had lived in the treatment facility who died, people who were younger than me. In all of these cases, one thought immediately came to my mind, "But for the grace of God, there I go."

I started to live life "one day at a time." At one time, I thought this a corny slogan, but it became a serious philosophy for me. Through prayer and meditation, I ask God to help me know what I should do each day and try to do those things that come to mind, I believe, through God's communication with me. As a thoughtful essay, entitled "One Day At a Time," says, it's the thought of yesterday and tomorrow that drive us mad, produce guilt, remorse, anxiety and worry.[2] If we live just for today, we begin to have serenity. What can I do now that will help others? That's something I can do right now. By taking a private inventory of my actions every night before going to sleep, I can identify where I failed to live up to the suggestions in the 12 steps of recovery and where I can improve my life. I can identify to whom I need to admit my mistakes and apologize for them. All of these activities are included in the 12 steps of recovery.

As I performed these activities on a daily basis, I noticed that my life began changing for the better. I felt peaceful inside, serene, and good things started to happen in my life, like job offers, financial security, loving family members, new friendships and more. Another AA slogan truly reflects my life then and now: "Nothing changes if nothing changes." By changing the way I lived my life every day, the consequences of how I lived changed too. I no longer woke up wondering what I had done the night before, smelling badly of alcohol. I could with confidence hold an intelligent conversation with people in the mornings, without worrying about whether or not I smelled of alcohol. A tremendous weight had lifted from my shoulders. I did not spend time figuring out how and when to get the alcohol I needed to get through a night of weekend. I became free.

What It's Like Now

I now live a fairly normal life. I am in recovery from the disease that gripped me for years and I am as free as a person can be after being imprisoned within my own body for nearly 30 years. No longer do I obsess about drinking alcohol and when the thought of taking a drink occurs to me, I pull out of that thought quickly. I want no part of that scene any more. I would not trade one sober day's serenity and peace for all of the excitement and euphoria of getting drunk again. God has blessed me and I am totally grateful that I did not meet any more disaster than I did while under the terrible influence of alcohol. I wake up each day and thank God for saving me and I spend a few minutes each night before falling asleep thanking God for my sobriety that day, asking Him for help in knowing His will for me and courage to carry that will out. I try to improve my time spent praying and meditating. The spiritual aspect of my life has changed dramatically and because of that, I feel much better than I have in a long time.

I can go into bars and clubs without craving alcohol. I can go to parties, spend hours talking to people and not drinking even if they are, and go home feeling much better than in the past when I left such parties very drunk. The obsession with getting alcohol has left me, I believe, because of my increasing spiritual "bank account." I recently attended a party that was a reunion of sorts; I knew most of the people there for over 20 years and I drank heavily with these people in the years when I socialized with them. The thought of taking a drink never occurred to me during that evening and most of them drank heavily. I found that I liked most of them as people, a thought that had never occurred to me before, as I had always concentrated on drinking at such parties, rather than on getting to know the people.

God has allowed me to move away from the highly competitive motives I had in the past and I now concentrate on being the best person I can be, rather than on being the best at whatever activity I engage in. This change has removed a great deal of stress from my life when I finish second or last at some competitive event. If I know I've tried my best, that's all that matters to me now. I apply this way of living to all of my affairs now and I discovered that the tremendous stress I used to feel to perform at a certain level is gone now that I have changed my attitude. The stress came from me, not from external circumstances, as I used to believe.

I've become humbler with time in this recovery program and I try to keep growing humbler. When I drank, I had paranoid delusions that a lot of people cared about what I did and how much I drank. I tried to hide my drinking from them. Today, I don't have to hide anything from anyone and that has led to a serenity and inner peace I never knew before. I do not run away from people or situations; I take God with me to help wherever I go. So far, He has not let me down.

I realize now that bad things still happen to me in life, but without alcohol to complicate things further, I can handle just about anything that happens. I believe that God has a plan for me that does not always include what I want at any given time, so when things don't go the way I think they should, I accept that God has something else in mind for me and whatever that is will be better than my idea. It's easier to accept things that way and not worry or form resentments about what's happened. I do not carry a load of guilt and fear around with me anymore. I am free.

I have my family back now (even though they remain cautious because they remember numerous promises to quit drinking in the past that I broke with regularity). I have a great job, several hobbies, and a bright future. But I also realize that I will lose all of this if I drink again. Nothing about drinking appeals to me any more; I'm not willing to risk what I have now by going back to drinking. I can never drink safely again and realizing that has made my life much easier than before.

I do many more things in my leisure time now than I could do when I drank. I read, jog, go to movies, concerts, and restaurants without hesitation, because I have lost the chains of active alcoholism. I do not fear police stopping me while driving nor do I have to make excuses for not accepting invitations to social events that I used to avoid because I couldn't drink there or because someone might catch on to how much I drank. I have a whole group of new friends in Alcoholics Anonymous, who genuinely care about me and who do not judge me as morally deficient, even after they've heard my story of the things I did while under alcohol's influence. I help others, particularly alcoholics seeking a solution to their problem, whenever

I can. I derive a great pleasure by giving without expecting to receive, even though I receive a good deal from these efforts.

By contrast to how my life was a few years ago, my life today is wonderful. I have no doubt that if I had found sobriety earlier, I would have many more pleasant memories than I now have, but I count my blessings every day; many alcoholics never find the solution and they go on to disastrous results, like prison, asylums, or death. The serenity I know today, free of the compulsion to drink, is better than any I ever knew before.

II
What I've Learned About Alcoholism

Doctor Silkworth's Opinion

In the book, *Alcoholics Anonymous,* a physician who treated a number of the earliest members of this group, Dr. Silkworth, wrote a letter expressing his support for the methods that AA used to gain sobriety. [3] In Dr. Silkworth's experience, many alcoholics who were otherwise helpless recovered through working the 12 steps of the AA recovery program. He writes about the disease of alcoholism in the terminology available to him in the 1930s and though more recent research has filled in many more details of both the physical and mental aspects of the disease, Dr. Silkworth's analysis still hits the mark very accurately. Alcoholics cannot take a single drink of alcohol without developing a craving for more. That power of that craving in alcoholics is beyond any human power to withstand. People who demonstrate great judgment, good sense and intellect in almost all other matters, become insanely selfish, dishonest, and irrational with respect to drinking alcohol. Even when serious personal and professional problems loom as a consequence of drinking, alcoholics cannot overcome the craving and we drink to disastrous results. Despite popular opinion, these drinking sprees do not represent weakness of will on the parts of alcoholics, rather they demonstrate the tremendous power of craving, which non-alcoholics do not experience. In other words, no one has sufficient will power to overcome the craving phenomenon, but most people do not experience this craving for alcohol, only alcoholics experience it.

Dr. Silkworth describes this craving phenomenon in the medical terminology of his day as a severe allergy to alcohol. In a curious way, he seems correct. Substances that most people can tolerate can produce horrendous conditions in others who cannot tolerate them, such as bee stings, pet dander, etc. Alcoholics react much differently to drinking alcohol than do non-alcoholics. Non-alcoholics reject drinking to excess because of the pain such an episode causes afterward. Alcoholics drink to excess repeatedly despite the pain these episodes cause afterward. Non-alcoholics employ the defense mechanism that most people have that motivates us to avoid painful situations once we've experienced the pain they produce when it comes to heavy drinking. Alcoholics do not have that defense mechanism regarding drinking. Alcoholics do feel pain as a result of over-drinking, but the euphoria we experience during a drinking episode overrides the memory of the pain experienced after all of the drunken sprees of the past and alcoholics drink excessively time and again in pursuit of that euphoria.

Alcohol is a mind-altering drug, which produces predictable affects on everyone who drinks it, alcoholic or non-alcoholic. Drinkers lose judgment, experience slow down in physical and mental reactions, loss of memory, reduced inhibitions and other common symptoms when drinking. The more alcohol consumed, the more exaggerated these symptoms become. Because alcohol depresses those who drink it, heavy drinkers have similar symptoms to manic depressive people. Ironically, the initial rush to euphoria tricks most alcoholics into believing that alcohol stimulates the body and mind and we crave that feeling. Despite every attempt that physicians, like Dr. Silkworth, could muster, they could not counter the phenomenon of craving alcohol. Practicing alcoholics have almost no hope of recovery through medical and psychiatric methods. Several Psychiatrists told me that they offered me no substantial hope; they suggested I join and actively participate in Alcoholics Anonymous, as the 12 step program of recovery held the only substantial hope of recovery for me. Dr. Silkworth's letters to the first two editions of the book, *Alcoholics Anonymous,* tell the same story. Having treated a number of the original contributors to that book, he remained amazed until he died the numbers of alcoholics who recovered by following the 12 steps, when all that medical science could muster had failed.[4]

Modern Research Results (Brain waves and chemistry)

When I went to in-patient treatment a few years ago, we watched a video that demonstrated the latest discoveries in medical science regarding the disease of alcoholism. The basic scientific question of why some people get addicted to alcohol and some do not formed the basis for the research about which this video concerned itself. The researchers discovered that the brain chemistry of known alcoholics differed considerably from that of known non-alcoholics. Specific brain chemicals, in particular, Endorphins, were missing or in low volumes in the brains of alcoholics when compared to the levels in the brains of non-alcoholics. In further tests, the scientists discovered that alcohol simulated the action of Endorphins in the brains of both alcoholics and non-alcoholics, i.e. the sensors that dictated production of the chemicals in brains reacted to alcohol in the same manner as they did for Endorphins. Since Endorphins make people feel mentally balanced and calm, the feeling for alcoholics, whose Endorphin level is usually low, is one of normalcy and balance. The desire to maintain that balanced feeling is the phenomenon that Dr. Silkworth called "craving" in his letters to *Alcoholics Anonymous*. When the brain stops producing Endorphins because the regulating sensors tell the production centers that enough are present, the manufacturing of these chemicals stops. Because alcohol evaporates rapidly, the balanced feeling rapidly fades and alcoholics drink more to regain and maintain the feeling. After the first dose of alcohol, though, the alcoholic will not achieve the same results during that drinking episode. The same effects occur in non-alcoholics.

Non-alcoholics emerge from their drinking episodes with a terrible feeling (hangover) that discourages them from drinking to intoxication again, or at least not frequently, because they do not want to experience the unbalanced feelings and pain that the withdrawal from alcohol produces in them. Alcoholics, on the other hand, feel unbalanced from low or no Endorphin production, so they crave the feeling of "serenity" that follows the initial drinking in a drinking episode and the pain of withdrawal associated with the "hangover" becomes endurable because it does not represent such a different feeling from their "normal" unbalanced feelings. Alcoholics then become addicted to the "normal" feeling and often begin drinking frequently enough that their neurological systems never completely free themselves from the effects of alcohol. In this stage of the disease, withdrawal from alcohol produces definite side effects of a negative variety, like tremors of the extremities, heavy perspiration, difficulty sleeping, etc. From this stage of the disease, more disastrous side effects occur as the alcoholic continues to drink heavily, including blackouts, unconsciousness, etc. Unable to function normally without alcohol, the alcoholic begins sneaking drinks at times when he/she knows he/she should not drink, such as on the job, to negate the withdrawal symptoms.

Alcoholism's Physical Symptoms and Damage to the Body

The disease progresses subtly in many alcoholics, so that movement from one stage to the next may take years to become apparent. The description of the alcoholic in *Alcoholics Anonymous*, written long before the brain chemistry experiments, accurately captures the external manifestations of these complex brain malfunctions. With respect to other matters, the alcoholic appears normal, reacting reasonably to most situations, but with regard to alcohol consumption, he/she becomes dishonest and possibly even dangerously anti-social.[5] By the time an alcoholic reaches the conclusion that he/she should stop drinking because of the problems drinking has caused in his/her life, he/she cannot stop drinking without outside help.

Twenty four years ago, my wife talked to me about stopping drinking because our relationship suffered from the frequency of my drinking episodes. I promised that I would stop drinking and meant that promise. But, the next day, I started drinking again without thinking about that promise until I had finished about half of my first drink. Even then, I could have washed the rest of the drink down the drain, but I continued drinking the rest of that evening, rationalizing that the next day would be a better day to stop drinking than that day. Unfortunately, the next day offered some other excuse to justify drinking and so on for the next 11 years. Though I had not thought of stopping drinking on my own, I had a really good reason to stop and could not. I had passed the point where my own

25

will power could have influenced whether or not I drank. I actually think now that from the time I started drinking, I might have lost the ability to "not drink" on my own volition.

I mentioned some of the withdrawal symptoms of alcoholism, but many alcoholics and the people closest to them miss many of the disease symptoms at a time when arresting the disease before major damage occurs may be possible. I list some of the more common symptoms that I exhibited early in my drinking career here, so that suffering alcoholics and their families, employers, and friends might recognize them and seek help. I rarely, if ever, had only one beer or mixed drink, when I started to drink. Two or more drinks characterized my drinking episodes from the beginning. That shows that I did not drink just to socialize, to fit in. I needed the amount of alcohol it took to produce the euphoria and that amount varied depending on how much I had eaten, how tired I felt, etc. I ignored the urgings of more experienced people, like my parents, who counseled me that I might drink too much when they lived in the proximity to observe me on a regular basis. I later drank despite my wife's protests and some of my friends.

When I felt stress, I turned to the bottle to feel relief. This practice, which I and many alcoholics used to justify drinking, actually indicates that I did not drink socially. I had evolved into a "problem drinker," drinking to escape problems or stressors. The colloquialism "partying" meant drinking to me; a party without alcohol did not count as a party, in my mind. Any recreational activity either involved or had the potential to involve alcohol consumption.

That included such activities as playing golf, going out to dinner, spending an evening with friends. As time went on, if I knew I might not get alcohol served at our destination, I took it with me. Hard liquor became preferable to me, because I got the feeling I craved quicker with this than with beer or wine, though if I could not get hard liquor, I would drink whatever form of alcohol made itself available. I hid the fact that I drank as heavily and frequently as I did, from my wife, my employers, and my friends. I tried to put up a façade that I didn't drink very much when I did drink a lot and often.

I decided to switch to drinking vodka at one point in my drinking career because I had heard that others cannot smell vodka on the breath. That way, I could continue drinking without concern that people would label me as a problem drinker or an alcoholic. Switching brands or types of alcoholic beverages for any reason indicates alcoholism, but I did not know that at the time. I made rules for myself about when I would drink and how much I would consume, thinking that not drinking in the mornings or never after a certain time in the evenings indicated that I did not have a problem with alcohol. Making rules for when and how much to drink clearly indicates alcoholism. Weekends afforded me the opportunities to call off the rules and I felt a relief that I could drink as much as I wanted without feeling guilty, also a strong symptom of alcoholism. Non-alcoholic people do not make rules about drinking; they never seriously think about it at all. They can take it or leave it alone.

As I became more tolerant of alcohol, i.e. I needed more alcohol to produce the same feeling that I craved, I became aware that the frequency with which I visited the liquor store might cause the employees there to brand me an alcoholic, so I started going to different places to buy the alcohol. This too strongly indicates alcoholism, as I would have just slowed down or quit drinking if I did not have a problem with it. The ways that I tried to deceive people about my drinking became more complicated, as I had to figure out ways to get new bottles into my house and get the empty bottles out undetected. Finally, I moved into another dimension with drinking when I discovered that taking a drink the first thing in the morning on weekends produced a great feeling that I could carry with me throughout the day just by periodically 'hitting the bottle." Because I hid these drinking episodes, I learned to stock up on bottles and hide them in various parts of the house. I also figured out that by replacing water with vodka in bottled water bottles, I could fool lots of people into believing that I had the healthy habit of hydrating myself throughout the day. Though I never did this at the office, on weekends and on trips, I carried a two liter water bottle filled with vodka wherever I went. For a time this worked well, I thought, as nobody ever challenged me about drinking alcohol. Unfortunately, some people knew what I did, but never said anything to me, so I believed that I got away with this insane behavior.

As time went on, my liver stopped adjusting to the ever increasing amounts of alcohol that I consumed and I started to appear as drunk as I really was after just a small amount of consumption. For several reasons, I managed to stop drinking for periods of time from one year to several months to several weeks, during these years. These droughts deceived me into believing that I did not have the alcoholic disease, because real alcoholics could not stop drinking for any reason. But, I always started drinking again, whenever the reason for stopping removed itself, which clearly indicates alcoholism. Despite a strong desire not to be an alcoholic, I was an alcoholic in denial for many years.

The most poignant examples of alcoholic symptoms started early in my drinking career and, like the disease itself, progressively got worse, occurring more frequently and with more disastrous results as time went on. These symptoms, pass outs and black outs, clearly represent the most serious and potentially most dangerous consequences of practicing alcoholism, since they lead directly to incarceration, commitment to insane asylums, loss of jobs, and, in the mind of the alcoholic sufferer, the fear of impending insanity. Passing out occurs when the body and mind stop functioning and the alcoholic becomes unconscious. Many alcoholics, me too, ended many of our days in this manner, passing out rather than sleeping. The old adage, "sleeping off" the drunkenness is a misnomer, because passed out alcoholics do not sleep. None of the rejuvenative processes that occur during sleep go on while the alcoholic is passed out and, as a result, we awake looking and feeling more fatigued than when we passed out. The red eyes that characterize people who abuse alcohol chronically result from this unconscious state. When we sleep, the brain goes through a series of events that cause physical processes, such as the eyes moving under their lids and tear ducts producing tears to lubricate the eyes as they move in this manner. But, when passed out, neither the movement nor the tear production occurs, so the alcoholic's eyes become seriously irritated and bloodshot in a manner different from such irritations as allergies or perspiration.

Black outs occur when the conscious part of the brain shuts down, but the body and other parts of the brain continue to function. Alcoholics in blackouts often do not even appear drunk, though their demeanors border on hyperactivity. Alcoholics in blackouts have murdered other people without remembering the act, driven hundreds of miles without remembering the drive, caused automobile accidents without remembering them and, more commonly, act foolishly at parties or aggressively toward family members with no recollection of these events. In the early stages of the disease, these blackouts usually become the topics of after action laughs, when people comment about the "crazy things" alcoholics did at the "party on Saturday night," but the alcoholic has no recollection of doing those "crazy things." We alcoholics usually minimalize these episodes as typical results of drunkenness, but they actually represent serious early indicators of alcoholism. Non-alcoholics do not have blackouts. In the more advanced stages of alcoholism, the blackouts often last for days or longer. I have no recollection of whole chunks of time from my past. Fear of what might have happened during these blackout periods haunted me often in my drinking days.

Besides these behavioral symptoms, alcoholics do real physical harm to our bodies while drinking. "Intoxication," the medical term for drunkenness, clearly indicates by etymology what we alcoholics do to ourselves when we drink. Alcohol is poison, "toxin," that damages almost every organ that it contacts on its journey through our digestive, neurological and respiratory systems. Long-range diseases that result from alcohol abuse include liver cirrhosis, artery blockages, various forms of cancer, and brain disorders. Most of these diseases that result from alcoholics continuing heavy drinking for many years would discourage and perhaps preclude some of us from drinking when we first started, if they occurred immediately after we began. But, they take a lot of time to develop and most of us are too far into the disease to stop on our own will power by the time we have symptoms or the realization hits us that we have put ourselves into real danger of developing these fatal diseases. So, we keep drinking. We are like frogs who if placed into a pot of boiling water, immediately jump out because of the pain and imminent danger, but when placed in a pot of tepid water will remain in the pot while the heat gradually increases through the boiling point until they die. The body adjusts to the heat gradually, so that the pain and warning of impending catastrophe from which the frog thrust into already boiling water immediately escapes, gets missed and the frog boils to death.[6]

The instances of alcoholics who have developed these terminal diseases indicate another symptom of the alcoholic disease. Often when we see them, they have physically failed to such a degree

31

that people who knew them earlier in life cannot believe that such a dramatic change has taken place in a seemingly short time. The explanation lies in the fact that most of us withdraw from social life as our drinking reaches serious proportions. We do not want to face chastisement for our drinking patterns, so we drink alone, closed in so others won't know. After a few years of such behavior, we have poisoned our bodies to the degrees that these other physical ailments set in and without us realizing it, we have become nearly unidentifiable as the same person people knew four or five years before. Alcohol accelerates the aging process, even if these serious internal diseases do not occur.

Alcoholism's Psychological/Emotional Symptoms and Damage to Others

Perhaps the most tragic aspect of alcoholism lays in the effects that happen to people other than the alcoholic himself/herself. Spouses, sons, daughters, parents, best friends, employers, and acquaintances get psychologically and emotionally hurt, nearly as badly as the alcoholic with this disease. *Alcoholics Anonymous* describes this phenomenon in very accurate detail. The practicing alcoholic acts like Dr. Jekyll and Mr. Hyde.[7] Those close to the alcoholic do not know which version of the person they love that will appear at any given time, the familiar one or the monster. We alcoholics have a penchant for destroying personal relationships, probably like no other type of person. The damage we cause, particularly to our children, goes well beyond anything we suffer, even in the most severe cases. Some of us die of the afflictions associated with our drinking, but to live with the emotional and psychological pain that loved ones are forced to live with must exceed death in the degree of misery experienced. Sadly, these innocent people often suffer from the same type of stubborn denial that we alcoholics endure while practicing.

Solid help is available in counseling and psychiatric services. Even more importantly for these co-dependents, the organizations called Al-Anon and Al-Ateen have formed to help these victims of the powerful disease through the same 12 step program of recovery that has saved so many alcoholics' lives. Many of these victims have told me that they learned through these programs that they were more ill than their alcoholic family members, exhibiting self-centeredness and delusional behavior to extreme degrees. Several attend AA meetings when meetings of their own groups are not readily available. The 12 steps help anyone with obsessive-compulsive disorders, no matter what the object of the obsession. Support groups have appeared to help obsessive-compulsive people recover from narcotic addiction (Narcotics Anonymous), cocaine addiction (Cocaine Anonymous), food addiction (Overeaters Anonymous), gambling addiction (Gamblers Anonymous), and more. The success of these groups provides a good deal of evidence to support the theory that addictions of all kinds follow the same patterns in development and in the process of recovery from them.

Alcoholism Is A Disease

In 1956, the American Medical Association declared alcoholism a disease, based on the conceptual theory of the criteria for diseases.[8] Like all diseases, alcoholism has specific symptoms, is chronic, progresses if not treated and is fatal. Though the individual circumstances surrounding each alcoholic's life differ, the symptoms of the disease do not vary. In 1939, when Dr. Silkworth first contributed his letter to *Alcoholics Anonymous,* he identified alcoholism as an allergy of the body, compounded by an obsession of the mind.[9] These medical terms indicate that a physician, well-educated in and experienced with the treatment of alcoholics, identified alcoholism as a disease long before the American Medical Association accepted it as such. The recent research that has led to the discovery of the genetic and chemical causes of the disease further supports the identification of alcoholism as a disease.

Recent philosophical endeavors, coupled with physical research, uncovered evidence that the nature of human beings is completely physical. In other words, the philosophical doctrine of dualism, human beings composed of two parts, body and soul, appears incorrect. If the mental states of humans are really brain processes, composed of neurons and chemical balances and imbalances, then the reasons for believing that we have a separate component, called the soul, disappear and the concept of human being becomes much simpler. Everything about us is physical. As we have just scratched the surface of the study of brain chemistry and its affects on human behavior, much remains for us to learn. But all discoveries in medical science point in this direction and these discoveries have important implications for moral judgments and revamping considerably legal and penal codes for humans, which I will discuss later.

Having identified alcoholism as a disease, researchers now can move toward finding a cure, if such a cure exists or if researchers can create one. But until a cure emerges, the alcoholic sufferer must employ the methods currently known to arrest the disease. The most difficult part of arresting the disease lies in the alcoholic him/herself. Before one can begin to recover, alcoholics must admit to themselves that they are alcoholics. But denial is one of the most common symptoms of the disease; despite the fact that most people who interact with an alcoholic know the truth, the alcoholic will pursue the delusion that he/she does not have this disease through enormous problems that alcohol obviously caused. This symptom shows how insane the alcoholic sufferer really is, as the alcoholic believes the lies that he/she tells others about the symptoms of drunkenness, extraordinary volumes of alcohol consumed, erratic behavior and withdrawal symptoms when alcohol is not available. With these physical symptoms, both when drinking heavily and when withdrawing from alcohol use, anyone paying attention and in a rational state of mind, can see the physical aspects of the disease. The psychological symptoms, though not as apparent, also show themselves in the behavior of the alcoholic. If anyone asks alcoholics about their drinking patterns, the alcoholics become irritated, often irate, and avoid discussing the subject. Once out of danger of confrontation and discovery, alcoholics rationalize their drinking to themselves, while thinking of ways to disparage and discredit the confronter.

Many alcoholics endure this phase of their diseases for many years, refusing to acknowledge that others know them better than they know themselves. During these times, the disease progresses. Alcoholics usually need to drink greater volumes of alcohol, more frequently to achieve the same feeling. The hangovers that accompany these drinking episodes get worse and last longer. As the disease progresses, alcoholics pay a greater physical price when they cannot get alcohol. Uncontrolled shaking, difficulty sleeping, uncontrolled sweating, inability to concentrate for more than a few minutes, and others, become more intense as the disease progresses. The emotional and psychological symptoms also become more intense. Alcoholics withdraw from social and loving relationships with their increased drinking. Family members, good friends and workplace associates threaten the exposure of the delusion, so alcoholics avoid contact with them whenever possible. Alcoholics stop engaging in activities that they formerly enjoyed, because they either cannot perform these activities while drinking or because other people do not drink while performing these activities. At work, alcoholics in advanced stages of the disease may function acceptably, but their behavior usually becomes erratic. Semi-aware that bosses and co-workers may learn of the extent of their drinking, alcoholics carefully hide their behavioral quirks, so that many work associates do not realize that alcoholics have a drinking problem until a major problem occurs, such as failure to show up when and where expected or a significant error in judgment or performance occurs. Once a large event comes to light, bosses and co-workers often piece together other evidence from insignificant episodes in the past that allow them to form a more complete picture of the extent to which alcohol affects the sufferers' lives.

Because discovery on the parts of employers, co-workers and family members means alcoholics must change their drinking patterns, they usually protect that secret passionately. The extent to which alcoholics hide the truth about how much and how often they drink amazes people without an alcohol addiction. Even more amazing to non-alcoholics, alcoholics themselves deny, rationalize or minimize how much and how often they drink to themselves. Non-alcoholics do not plan drinking sprees, do not hide alcohol in places where family, friends, bosses and co-workers will not find it, do not alter plans in order to drink, and do not obsess about where and when the next drink will come from. All of these symptoms of the psychological part of the disease are common among alcoholics and the fact that some alcoholics do not have all of these symptoms, does not mean they are not alcoholics. If alcoholics continue to drink for extended periods of time, they will eventually manifest all of these symptoms.

Medical professionals, recovering alcoholics and family members of all alcoholics often speak and write about insanity when describing the practicing alcoholic. This assessment hits the mark directly; when we alcoholics drink, we are insane. As time goes on in our drinking lives, the consequences of drinking become so distressful that any rational person would immediately determine the causes of his/her problems as alcohol and quit drinking on the spot. But alcoholics do not do this; despite lost families, lost jobs, arrests, personal isolation, hospitalization and other terrible consequences, alcoholics will continue to drink, blaming their troubles on other people, bad luck or some other external cause. In most cases, alcoholics who have experienced these consequences still believe that they control their drinking and start on the next drinking episode with the idea that it will turn out better than the last time. Sometimes this happens, but eventually, worse consequences follow and usually these happen in the not too distant future from the last debacle. If insanity means doing the same things over and over, while expecting different results, then alcoholics fit that definition to a tee. In many cases, alcoholics end up in insane asylums because they have lost all touch with reality.

As *Alcoholics Anonymous* states, alcoholics often exhibit rational and normal reasoning and reactions with respect to all other aspects of their lives.[10] But, once alcohol gets introduced into their lives, they react irrationally, abnormally, selfishly, anti-socially and insanely. We alcoholics often have a great deal of ability, intelligence, and promise for the future. When not drinking, many of us have become quite successful in business, in academics, athletics and other walks of life. But practicing alcoholics who progress in their diseases soon find that the effort needed to drink as much as they need to drink and continue to successfully execute their careers becomes more than they can muster. Sometime before this point in the progression of the disease, alcoholics have already lost the ability to manage a family, a career, a normal social life and a drinking career. Families almost always feel the pinch first, because they live with the alcohol abuser and feel the direct sting of the disease before anyone else, aside from the alcoholic.

The fact that we alcoholics display ability when not drinking clearly shows that alcoholism is a progressive disease of the body and mind. No sane person would sacrifice everything worth having in life, health, family, friends, careers, for a mind-altering substance. Nobody chooses to do this of his/her free will; the disease causes alcoholics to fail to recognize the disasters that alcohol causes in their lives at the same time that it's causing them. We read in *Alcoholics Anonymous*, that alcohol is "cunning, baffling, powerful" to alcoholics.[11] Indeed, it is. It tells us we are okay at the same time it robs us of all of these wonderful benefits of life. As we often hear said in AA meetings and other places, we alcoholics are not bad people trying to be good; we are sick people trying to get well. Practicing alcoholics just have not yet realized that they are sick and the degree to which they are sick. If we live long enough, some of us realize this in time to change our lives and recover from this terrible disease. Unfortunately, many alcoholics die before they realize this.

Fortunately, some of us do recover. I described how I am able to continue in recovery earlier. My individual program of recovery may not work for others, but the common thread in the programs of every recovering alcoholic with whom I have talked is working the

12 step program. The first step, "We admitted we were powerless over alcohol, that our lives had become unmanageable," is the most critical of the steps if an alcoholic is to recover. Any delusion that we alcoholics can ever drink safely, without the terrible consequences that getting drunk causes us, "must be smashed," in the words of *Alcoholics Anonymous*.[12] The first step means to me that I can never safely take a single drink of alcohol again. Internalizing that maxim is crucial to successfully working the other steps, because without that realization, most of us have no incentive to change our lives, which the 12 step program requires. If I cannot drink safely ever again, I must make the changes in my life that will help to ensure that I never take another drink. For alcoholics, such a change is humongous. But once we've taken that first step, truly believing that we can never drink safely again and wanting to stay sober, the changes that we make yield more spectacular consequences for us than most of us could ever have imagined. We adopt a spiritual way of living, trusting a higher power, the nature and attributes of which do not matter. We humble ourselves to become totally honest with ourselves, acknowledging all the people we hurt while drinking and all of the negative feelings we carried around with us for the duration of our drinking careers. We pray daily and we freely admit to a trusted person all of the harm we caused, as we remember it. We decide to mend the fences we've damaged in the wakes of our drinking careers and go out to admit to those we hurt that we were wrong. We then try to help other people, especially suffering alcoholics who need our experience, strength and hope.

By putting ourselves behind everyone else in consideration, we achieve a freedom and happiness we never knew before. As many of us describe it, we are reborn.

III
Common Misperceptions About Alcoholism

Weakness of Will

For centuries, most people made judgments about alcoholics that result from not understanding alcoholism as a disease and the illogical process of judging other people entirely from their own experiences. I do not intend to analyze in detail the causes of these phenomena, but to highlight some of the more common myths concerning alcoholism and explain the true nature of the disease attendant to them. If the belief in these myths hurt nobody, I would not waste time doing so. However, believing these myths hurts many people, including the alcoholic, the alcoholic's family, the people with whom the alcoholic has personal and social relationships and the alcoholic's employer and co-workers.

In several instances, I have heard people who have the potential to influence the beliefs of others, such as radio and television personalities, business managers, none of whom possess authoritative knowledge on the subject, say that they do not accept alcoholism as a disease. The perpetuation of this mistaken belief hurts society, in general, by blocking progressive thinking and planning about arresting the disease and solving the multitude of problems created by alcoholics.

People who openly discard the scientific theory, confirmed by observation, that alcoholism is a disease make the logical error of judging another category of people by their own experiences. As a person who has never suffered from cancer, I cannot logically judge those who have cancer by my experiences. Similarly, those who do not suffer from alcoholism, cannot logically judge those who do on the basis of non-alcoholic experience. However, just as epileptics were sometimes burned at the stake during the Middle Ages because physicians could find no explanation for their seizures other than possession by the devil, without the recent research into brain chemistry, physicians could not explain alcoholism without reference to weakness of will power. Just as epileptics suffered unjust persecution in the Middle Ages, alcoholics have suffered unjust persecution and faulty moral judgments about them for centuries. The next discussion centers of a few of these common myths.

The first myth blames the alcoholic for weakness of will. In other words, many people, including many alcoholics themselves, believe that people who drink alcoholically do so voluntarily; they choose to do so. If humans have free will, and the debate over whether we do or do not has gone on in philosophical and religious circles for centuries, we must have an unobstructed choice between alternative courses of action, moral responsibility for which can logically be assigned to the person who makes these free choices. If a person freely chooses one course of action over another or several others in a given situation, then others may rationally judge that choice on moral grounds. The action chosen is morally right, morally wrong or morally neutral. Because non-alcoholic people believe they have freedom of choice over drinking or not drinking alcohol (I do not think they do), they often assume that alcoholics also make a similar free choice and therefore subject themselves to moral judgments. The main logical fallacy lies in the assumption of choice on the part of alcoholics; but, a secondary fallacy lies in the assumption that non-alcoholics freely choose to drink or not drink alcohol.

Alcoholics, whose brain chemistry differs from non-alcoholics' brain chemistry, do not choose to drink or not to drink once the chemical process alcohol triggers in the mind begins. The process of choice has gone from the practicing alcoholic's mind and will. The obsession and compulsion to drink grow more powerful over time and, over the course of a long time, they overcome every aspect of the alcoholic's life.

This process progresses gradually, in most cases, so that the initial stages of alcoholism usually pass by without anyone, especially the alcoholic, noticing the symptoms. Only in the later stages of the disease, when alcoholics stand nearly no chance of stopping drinking for a considerable period of time or completely, that others notice the symptoms. Because of the myths surrounding alcoholism, those who notice these symptoms often fail to do anything about them, as to do so would be to brand a loved one or a close friend as a morally deficient person. If the same people noticed symptoms of another disease in their loved one or friend, they would most likely speak to the victim or to someone who might help the victim seek medical attention. No moral stigma attaches to such diseases, but since alcoholism is often misunderstood as a moral condition, rather than a medical condition, people find it easier to ignore the symptoms than to confront them.

The stories of thousands of alcoholics during their drinking days argue strongly against the misperception of an alcoholic's weakness of will. Most of us have gone to extraordinary extremes to get alcohol when we drank, demonstrating a far greater will power than most people exhibit in their lives. Some have driven over a hundred miles to find an open liquor store. I paid a taxi driver $65 on one occasion to drive me to an open liquor store on a Sunday when I could not drive my car there. I would not have paid that much money for a ride to a grocery store if I had been hungry and had no food in the house. Under the compulsion to drink, we alcoholics will do nearly anything to get alcohol, to include lying, cheating and stealing. Most of us would rarely lie, cheat or steal in other circumstances; but the power alcohol exerts over us overwhelms us when we reach this stage of the disease. In fact, I believe that this power overwhelms us long before we reach the latter stages of the disease, but the amounts of alcohol needed to produce the euphoria our brains crave is much lower in the early stages of the disease, so we do not need to lie, cheat or steal to get the amount of alcohol we need.

As mentioned earlier, alcoholics under the influence of alcohol cannot logically be said to be sane. We do insane things to get alcohol, while drinking alcohol and, especially late in the disease, while in alcohol-induced blackouts. As our laws accurately reflect, people who do not rationally and freely choose between alternative courses of action are not rationally subject to moral and legal judgments. This legal distinction is based on the Normative Ethical principle that "Ought implies can."[13] To say that a person ought to perform an action implies that he/she can perform that action. Alcoholics, still engulfed in the powerful compulsion to drink alcohol, cannot refuse to drink without stringent intervention. If temporary insanity exists, then practicing alcoholics certainly are temporarily insane.

People associated with practicing alcoholics should treat them as sick people, as that is just what they are. I realize the difficulty in dealing with an irrational person, which practicing alcoholics certainly are, but to attempt to influence the alcoholic to change behavior based on guilt or fear is to fail miserably. The alcoholic does not feel these emotions about drinking alcohol; often we feel them about actions we perform when drunk and in alcoholic blackouts, but not about drinking itself. We feel guilt about not controlling our drinking or our behavior when drunk, but not about drinking. Also, because alcohol clouds our perceptions and judgment, we often cannot comprehend the seriousness of our condition, even when others see it plainly and point it out to us.   However, one chance for successful intervention lies with a recovering alcoholic speaking to a practicing alcoholic, one-on-one, recounting experiences from the recovering alcoholic's past and demonstrating that an alcoholic can recover from the illness, no matter how far into the disease the practicing alcoholic has progressed. Sometimes substance abuse treatment professionals can successfully intervene, as well, but their chances of reaching the practicing alcoholic fall short of those of a recovering alcoholic. Practicing alcoholics relate to the experiences of recovering alcoholics in a way that someone who has not gone through the same experiences cannot hope to achieve.

Only when an alcoholic has "dried out," been free from any alcohol for a substantial period of time, weeks or months, can he/she begin to view the past accurately. Once alcoholics view their past experiences with a clear mind and realize the central role alcohol has played in the downward spiral of their fortunes, they can begin to focus on not drinking and reconstructing their lives. More on how to do this will follow. For now, successfully challenging the myth of alcoholism as a weakness of will suffices as the main point of this section.

Legal Issues with the Weakness of Will Myth

In theory, laws reflect morality; however, in reality, laws do not always reflect morality. A number of historical examples of great importance support this observation, such as the legality of slavery within a number of great civilizations, concentration camps, etc. As with everything in human experience, our knowledge evolves as our powers of observation increase and the amount of time knowledgeable people spend applying these powers to the problems of life increases. We change our beliefs based on new discoveries all of the time and, historically, we have changed our laws based on discoveries that have altered our knowledge about human behavior. Our laws accurately capture the basis of Normative Ethics in the "ought implies can" principle. Courts do not try people who appear not to make free, rational choices about their actions. We do not punish insane people or those who have committed illegal actions while under some form of coercion. They have not acted "freely."

I believe that actions performed by alcoholics and people addicted to other mind-altering substances should fall into a similar category. The fact that laws do not protect the rights of such sick people indicates a failure of communication between different segments of society. A number of medical professionals have told me over the years that I have a serious, even fatal, illness called alcoholism. With the proper treatment, I can arrest the disease, but I can never expect cure. Like hypertension or diabetes, the trick for the alcoholic lies in learning to live with it. But the mental part of the disease itself fights against accepting the diagnosis of medical professionals and many alcoholics perpetuate the delusion that they do not have the disease through incredible instances of hardship and even death. The failure of the medical community to educate the legal community about the nature of alcoholism as a disease or the failure of the legal community to learn about alcoholism as a disease perpetuates an injustice.

The fact that laws prohibit driving drunk, public appearances while drunk, and other such activities while drunk indicates this dramatic miscommunication to a great degree. I am either very sick or I am not. If I am, then I should not be legally culpable for actions performed while drunk that I clearly did not make a free, rational choice to perform. If I am not sick, then I am morally responsible for actions that occur during a period of drunkenness. But given that I cannot even remember most of the actions I performed when drunk, how is it possible that I freely and rationally chose to perform those actions? I argue it makes no sense to claim that I ought not to have performed those actions, since I did not make a free, rational choice. Also, I argue that while any vestige of alcohol remains in my system, I will have an overwhelming compulsion to drink more alcohol, as any addict has the overwhelming compulsion to indulge in the addictive substance, food, nicotine, caffeine, etc. that removes any chance of making a free, rational choice about using the substance.

The myth associated with the legal judgments reflected in current laws that much of the population accept is that behavior covered by a law should be covered by a law. In other words, the fact that driving drunk is illegal means that all who do so must freely choose to do so. Such a judgment clearly stems from the mistaken belief that the study of the law means the study of morality. The fact that lawyers know the law does not mean that they know morality. The fact that lawyers study law does not mean that they know medicine, neurology, chemistry, or the other subjects that define alcoholism as a disease. Even more importantly, the people who make laws in democratically elected legislatures do not have to have studied law, medicine or any other particular discipline. They often accept commonly held misconceptions about alcoholism and addictions and vote for legislation accordingly. If the successes of medical treatments for alcoholics and other addictive diseases argue against making and enforcing laws that treat sick people unfairly.

Moral Depravity

In competitive societies, people fairly routinely compare themselves to others with an eye toward superiority. As the average person can rarely point to superior physical or intellectual attributes, he/she often reverts to a commonly misunderstood comparison, moral superiority or inferiority, to make himself/herself feel superior to others. Because most people do not study ethics seriously, few people challenge these judgments with a substantial basis and this form of delusional behavior, thinking oneself morally superior to others, goes on routinely. Since most non-alcoholic people mistakenly believe that they choose freely between drinking alcohol or not, or how much they drink when they do drink alcohol, they easily move to the mistaken assumption that they have a moral superiority over those who get drunk or drink frequently. But since morally relevant actions must occur as a result of free choice and alcoholics do not freely choose to drink or get drunk, the idea that alcoholics are morally depraved is erroneous. To correctly receive a moral judgment concerning my actions, I must have a free choice, thus be "in my right mind;" but, I am not in "my right mind" when I drink. In fact, my mind plays no role in the process of drinking and getting drunk at all, at least, not in any sense that means that I rationally thought about my options and without coercion chose to drink over not drinking.

History gives us multiple examples of the fallacious reasoning that goes into these types of judgments, whereby individual persons use their personal experiences, motives, and/or perceptions to make huge leaps in logic to infer that everyone else (or almost everyone else) has had the same experiences, motives, and/or perceptions. Countries and groups of countries have fought wars due this failure in reasoning. The concentration camp mentality, that allows authorities to imprison whole groups of people based on race, nationality, religion, etc. exemplifies this logical error.

The fallacy, as it applies to non-alcoholics judging alcoholics, roughly aligns with Caucasians judging Blacks or other races or to men judging women's actions or Americans judging Palestinians. The experiences, motives, and/or perceptions of any individual cannot logically apply to any whole group of people to which the individual does not belong. In fact, the experiences, motives, and/or perceptions of any individual cannot logically apply to everyone in the group to which the individual making the judgment belongs. Experiences, motives and perceptions belong completely to the individual person. No one else knows for sure why any other person

51

acted the way he/she acted and no one can correctly assume that if he/she found himself/herself in the exactly the same situation, that he/she would act any differently than the target of the judgment.

This fallacy, sometimes called a form of the "problem of induction," becomes especially serious in nature when laws protect the fallacy and punish innocent people who violate them. The fact that we do not put known insane people in prison for their actions when not totally in control of their reasoning faculties demonstrates that a faulty thinking process applies to the formulation of laws related to alcoholics who drink alcohol. Most alcoholics who spend a night in jail and pay a minor fine for a "drunk in public" conviction have no more freely chosen to do this than the epileptic chooses to have a seizure or the coronary patient chooses to have cardiac arrest.

Some magistrates and judges have apparently reached the conclusions that the alcoholic in these situations chose to drink, rather than not drink, and so becomes responsible for the consequences of behavior when drunk. But, alcoholics do not freely choose to drink or not to drink, even with regard to the first drink in a drinking episode. Even if we did freely choose between taking the first drink and not taking the first drink, that does not mean that we freely chose to get drunk and clearly did not choose to pass out on the park bench or stumble wildly across the street, etc., the actions for which we get arrested. The night in jail provides no deterrent to the alcoholic, who cannot discern that he/she has no control over alcohol. Having gotten drunk numerous times in the past and not gotten arrested, the alcoholic, in a mind-fog, usually thinks he/she had a run of bad luck associated with being in the wrong place at the wrong time. Putting an epileptic in jail during a seizure makes about as much sense as putting an alcoholic in jail while drunk. Nothing gets resolved with the alcoholic's or epileptic's disease and he/she pays an unjustified fine.

Fear of the Unknown

Closely associated with the problem of induction, another problem presents itself under close scrutiny. Since practicing alcoholics can become dangerously anti-social when drinking, other people fear them. Not understanding alcoholism as a disease, non-alcoholics, out of fear, demand that legislative and judicial means be applied to solve this medical problem. Perhaps fear motivates us all in the most powerful ways, but, as fear is a negative emotion, it can adversely cloud the reason and cause us to act irrationally. I know a number of people who will not fly in commercial aircraft in the aftermath of the terrorist attacks on September 11, 2001. Such a fear of flying based on those terrible events shows how fear can cloud the reason and motivate irrational actions. In fact, had anyone of these same people flown on September 11th in another aircraft aside from the four hi-jacked planes and at the same time as the hi-jackings, they still would have been safer in the air than driving a car on the ground. Flying is much safer than driving; every statistic indicates the truth of this fact. Yet irrational fears keep many potential passengers from making rational choices regarding flying versus driving even three years after the terrorist attacks.

Similarly, fear of the alcoholic, the ugly, mean, dirty bum, prevents non-alcoholics from attempting to find the cause of the problem and address it. Arresting drunks gets them off the streets temporarily, but by no means begins to solve the problems that will emerge again and again when an alcoholic drinks. Many people pass a drunk who has passed out on a park bench or propped up against the wall of a building and react with disgust and disdain. But the same person who reacts so judgmentally toward the alcoholic would stop to help another person who had lost consciousness and fallen to the ground. At least, that person would call the police for help or call an ambulance, but the misconception that the alcoholic has freely chosen his/her fate causes the person who should help the sick person, to ignore the victim. Though drunks often exhibit aggressive behavior when intoxicated, they seldom really hurt people, since their equilibrium and coordination usually have disappeared because of the debilitating effects of alcohol. The alcoholic generally poses no direct threat to anyone else. To ignore such a sick person in public would in other cases be considered negligent. To walk away from a person who had fainted on the sidewalk might bring criminal charges to the negligent person, but not so with alcoholics, who often have achieved exactly the same state of unconsciousness as the person who fainted.

Fear breeds anger, contempt and clamor for action. Because most people wrongly judge that alcoholics have brought their conditions on themselves, the clamor for action usually takes the form of law enforcement. Alcoholics get arrested, charged with crimes and fined or imprisoned. Judges tell alcoholics that their fines or jail time should serve as deterrents from such future incidents, but since alcoholics do not freely choose to drink, the punishments have no bearing on whether or not the alcoholic drinks again. On occasion, such an encounter with the law becomes the last straw in a series of events that cause the alcoholic to seek help. But, most times, the alcoholic has not connected his/her drinking with the problems he/she has had and will turn to alcohol again as soon as an opportunity arises. Because of this, non-alcoholics think very lowly of alcoholics, as people who have disdain for the law. But, usually, alcoholics do not disdain the law; they just cannot stop drinking on their own volition and employ a variety of delusional reasoning processes to ignore the fact that alcohol causes them to lose complete control over their actions. Until they can get honest with themselves, this pattern of behavior will continue. Fear of the unknown prevents many non-alcoholics from directly intervening in a positive way in the lives of practicing alcoholics.

IV.
What's Wrong with Common Misperceptions About Alcoholism

No Free Will Involved

As *Alcoholics Anonymous* points out, alcoholics have lost the ability to choose between drinking and not drinking.[14] The power of will that alcoholics often display in other areas of their lives becomes non-existent when alcohol enters the picture. The phenomenon of craving alcohol that all alcoholics experience becomes all consuming for practicing alcoholics and even a strong desire to stop drinking does not prevent the beginning of another drinking episode and its attendant debacle. Just as diabetics do not choose to go into shock due to unbalanced blood sugar levels, so alcoholics do not choose to start or continue a drinking episode. They have no power over the cravings. Even when some powerful deterrent intervenes to prevent a practicing alcoholic from drinking, like the threat of job termination, travel to an area where alcohol is not available, the craving for alcohol continues. The practicing alcoholic pays a tremendous physical and mental price when out of reach of a drink. Some actually die from withdrawal, a characteristic of the disease that makes alcoholism more dangerous than other addictions.

My personal experiences, the stories of hundreds of alcoholics I have heard and the medical facts about the physical/mental characteristics of the alcoholic addiction strongly indicate to me that alcoholics do not exercise free will over drinking or not drinking alcohol. Even more apparent, the actions that practicing alcoholics perform when under the influence of alcohol do not meet the criteria of free will choices. Because of this, moral judgments to these actions cannot properly apply. Even if we assume that an alcoholic chooses to take the first drink that will almost certainly result in a series of drinks and eventual drunkenness, to judge that he/she has done something morally wrong by taking that first drink, would imply that anyone who chooses to take a drink of alcohol has done something morally wrong. Persons skeptical about accepting alcoholism as a disease might also argue that non-alcoholics do not perform a morally wrong action by taking a drink, because their history does not indicate that they will lose control over their faculties and leave havoc in their wakes, as most alcoholics do. But, practicing alcoholics do not realize the degrees to which alcohol encompasses their lives when they drink. They, like non-alcoholics, do not identify the taking of a drink of alcohol as a catalyst to violence, negligence, and anti-social behavior. The delusion from which practicing alcoholics suffer prevents them from perceiving the truth about their situations. They no more commit a crime by taking the first drink than the non-alcoholic.

The extent of the belief in the myth of alcoholics' ability to choose between drinking and not drinking alcohol amazes me. Some physicians, not specially educated in treating alcoholism; some judges and lawyers, specially trained in the impertinence of the law to insane people, and some others in authority believe the myth to some extent, if not entirely. The results of these misconceptions are far-reaching and destructive. Practicing alcoholics who have not had the benefit of learning the truth about their diseases or who still delude themselves into believing they do not have a drinking problem believe the myth themselves, because authority figures say and do things that indicate they believe the myth. Alcoholics who should seek treatment sometimes shy away from it because of guilt based in the false belief that they have a choice over drinking or not drinking. Physicians recommend treatments that will not work in the vast majority of cases, because alcoholics cannot just stop drinking on the word of a physician. Judges impose sentences on alcoholics with the caveat that the judge wants to help the alcoholic stay sober through fear by punishing him/her, wrongly assuming that alcoholics choose to drink and will "think twice" about it if they have the threat of additional punishment hanging over their heads. None of these ploys work, because alcoholics do not exercise free will in regard to drinking or not drinking. Guilt and fear only work as motivation when a person makes a choose freely over his/her actions. Alcoholics do not make such a choice regarding alcohol, but suffer further consequences when they drink after physicians and judges tell them not to drink. The suffering alcoholic earns the misconceived reputation as morally depraved and alcoholics, in general, get this undeserved reputation hung on them. We are not bad people trying to be good; we are sick people trying to get well.

Laws Do Not Address the Problem and Are Unjust

While I do not advocate drunk driving, domestic violence, failure to pay just debts, professional dishonesty or any of the other common incidents in which practicing alcoholics commonly become involved when drunk, I strongly believe that the solutions to these problems do not lie in legislation. I have heard various statistics on the percentages of people serving extended prison sentences who were either drunk or high when they perpetrated the crimes for which they are incarcerated. From one person I heard that 80% of these inmates were drunk or high and from others I have heard that 60% fell into this category. In either case, a large percentage of those locked up for a long time appear to have a problem with substance abuse. The problems of prison overcrowding and failure of the rehabilitative process in prisons might be mitigated if we plan to treat what appears as the real problem: addictive disease rather than crime.

While standing laws protect the rights of insane people accused of committing criminal acts, leaving alcoholics and drug addicts out of that category, given what we have learned about these addictive diseases, seemingly violates the civil rights of this large group of people. In some States, changes in laws seem to reflect this understanding of alcoholism as a disease rather than a character defect, but in others, driven by misunderstanding, the laws have changed to impose harsher sentences for drunk driving, public intoxication, etc. Preventing alcoholics from driving, as a number of States have implemented through a number of devices, reflects the educated approach to solving that problem. But, the misunderstanding displayed in other States, where increased legal penalties have come to pass, involves the myth that alcoholics freely choose to drink or not drink and that fear of stiffer penalties will reduce the incidences of these events. While such increased penalties may deter non-alcoholics from drinking and driving, etc., they will have no bearing on alcoholics, who probably make up the majority of such offenders. Few people get caught drunk driving; mostly people who habitually drink and drive get caught and people who drink that often are usually alcoholics. Also, alcoholics convicted under these laws will pay dearly for having a disease over which they have no control unless they have sought and accepted treatment. Failure to classify actions performed by alcoholics while under the influence of alcohol as insanity will result in even more severe unjust punishments.

I believe the solution lies in a better education about the progression of the disease and the steps that people other than the alcoholics themselves can take to promote recovery from the disease, while at the same time preventing alcoholics from hurting other people while in the practicing phase of the disease. Alcoholics not in recovery will get drunk over and over, will black out and perform negative actions of which they are not aware while performing them, go through legal processes that cost taxpayers a lot of money, and not come out any less likely to do the same things again.

The problems are not legal; they are medical. Most alcoholics with criminal histories would never have done the things that got them in trouble with the law if they had not been drunk. The numbers of alcoholics with multiple criminal offenses attests to this assessment. If the alcohol problem gets solved, then the criminal problem gets solved. Many prisons host groups of Alcoholics Anonymous and some have psychological treatment available, but inmate alcoholics tend to deny their diseases, just as those outside prison do. Without turning their alcoholic lives around, many alcoholic inmates will turn to drink again upon release from prison and the same patterns of criminal activities, usually while in an alcohol induced blackout will follow. If the alcohol problem does not get resolved, neither will the criminal problem.

Moral Judgments Do Not Apply

Many alcoholics never get in trouble with the law. However, most practicing alcoholics have trouble in their lives. The homes of actively using alcoholics suffer first and most from the behavior of the practicing alcoholic. The myth that alcoholics make free will choices to drink often severely complicates an already difficult situation in the families of alcoholics. Spouses, parents, siblings and other persons who share households with practicing alcoholics, in many cases, do not know that alcoholism is a disease that renders the alcoholic incapable of choosing to stop drinking. Judging the alcoholic by their own perceived choices in this regard, non-alcoholic family members usually hold their alcoholic family members in moral contempt. Initially, the lethargy and emotional withdrawal that alcohol abuse causes appear as the symptoms of this disease. Later in the progression of the disease, alcoholics become emotionally abusive toward other family members and usually do not intend to do so nor are they aware that they have done so. In some cases, the emotional abuse reverts to physical abuse, again not a conscious choice on the parts of the alcoholics, whose mental faculties have become warped by long term exposure to alcohol and whose emotions become skewed by the high volumes of toxic chemicals in their bodies. All of these symptoms breed emotional instability, fear, anger and other negative feelings in the non-alcoholic family members. The worst part about these situations arises from the belief on the parts of the non-alcoholic family members that the alcoholic family member chooses to feel and behave this way by choosing to drink.

The lying, cheating and stealing that alcoholics do while under the influence of alcohol, though abominable in the damage they do to family members, are not typical of the morally depraved types of behavior to which we attach negative moral judgments. People who intentionally try to take advantage of other innocent people by lying, cheating and stealing should be judged from the moral standpoint. But alcoholics, who neither make free choices nor plan their actions and the subsequent consequences through clear reasoning processes, are not logically subject to the same moral judgment process.

Many non-alcoholic family members, as well as other people, make moral judgments about the actions of their alcoholic family member or associate. Initially, these judgments result from misunderstanding of the alcoholic's condition as a disease, over which he/she exercises no control. But, in some cases, even after medical professionals instruct family members about the nature of the disease and the fact that alcoholics cannot help having the disease, the non-alcoholic family members cling to the idea that they are morally superior to the alcoholic family member. This belief in moral superiority manifests itself in demanding of the alcoholic more than one can reasonably expect, based on the mistaken belief that the alcoholic owes a debt to the people who have borne the brunt of the alcoholic's sprees, i.e. emotional abuse, dereliction of responsibility, etc. The truth is that the alcoholic's disease has rendered him/her incapable of making free will choices of action and since he/she is incapable of maliciousness of intention, no moral judgment applies to the actions performed when drunk.

Another difficulty in the complicated web that alcohol weaves in human interactions arises with the family members of practicing alcoholics. They become ill during the years of drinking on the parts of the alcoholics in their lives. Many of the same symptoms that alcoholics exhibit come out in their non-alcoholic family members, especially children who learn behavior patterns from their parents. The syndrome called, "The Adult Child of an Alcoholic," is real and calls for separate treatment for the family members so afflicted. I know this from a personal standpoint, as I am also the adult child of an alcoholic, as well as an alcoholic. A book written on the subject, entitled, *The Adult Child of an Alcoholic,* lists 14 symptoms of this disease.[15] Whether or not the child of an alcoholic becomes an alcoholic, he/she will still have most of these symptoms because of the exposure to an alcoholic parent in the formative years. Though children rarely understand the negative impact they are experiencing by living with a practicing alcoholic, they find difficulties later in life dealing with long term relationships and other things that children who have not lived with an alcoholic parent do not experience.

Alcoholics cannot reasonably take moral responsibility for any of these developments. Again, since alcoholics do not freely choose to drink nor do they freely make choices in actions when under the influence of alcohol, none of the terrible consequences of alcoholism has a moral connotation to them. Though difficult for some family members of alcoholics to practice, they should treat their alcoholic family member as he/she really is: a very sick person. Understanding and compassion may help the alcoholic, whereas confrontation and moral degradation will certainly not work. In the end, everyone in the families of practicing alcoholics needs professional help to get better. *Alcoholics Anonymous,* describes this aspect of the disease accurately: no other disease affects so many other people in so many adverse ways as alcoholism does.[16] The alcoholic is like a tornado, destroying everything in its path while it rages. The truth of this claim argues well for more and better treatment for everyone affected by the disease. Many an innocent child's life has turned upside down as a result of a parent's alcoholism.

V.
Correct Perceptions About Alcoholism

Sick People Who Need Help

I have already enumerated the physical and mental symptoms of the disease, but the practical matter remains for resolution, how do spouses, parents, children and associates of alcoholics handle living with an alcoholic. Practicing alcoholics often rank among the most difficult people with whom to deal in the world. Our personalities change dramatically depending on whether or not we have alcohol in our bodies and, if we do, how much is present. *Alcoholics Anonymous* describes these mood swings accurately by referring to the Dr. Jekyll and Mr. Hyde contrast that really exemplifies our behavior.[17] Because we become anti-social and often belligerent while drunk, we isolate ourselves from those who least deserve the abuse we tend to dish out and who have the best chance (among non-alcoholics) of helping us recover. Fear of what might happen if they confront us while drunk keeps many family members from approaching us at all. Children, who have experienced the embarrassment of their alcoholic parent appearing drunk in front of friends, stop inviting friends to the home, to avoid similar episodes in the future. Spouses find excuses to leave home to avoid arguments and often develop a habit of refusing social invitations for fear of the alcoholic spouse showing up drunk or becoming disgustingly drunk at the party.

In many cases, when non-alcoholic family members ask the alcoholic member why he/she got drunk, the response places blame on the questioner or on the other non-alcoholic family members. Sometimes the non-alcoholic family members actually believe that they are to blame, but they have no blame in this matter at all. Other times, the practicing alcoholic will offer excuses dealing with job stress or other external factors that many people, alcoholics and non-alcoholics alike, accept due to ignorance about the disease. As *Alcoholics Anonymous* points out, though, alcoholics themselves do not know why they got drunk, any more than the family member who asks the question.[18] We drink because we are alcoholics and for no other reason. We crave the feeling of euphoria that alcohol provides and that craving becomes so intense that we will pursue its satisfaction to the detriment of personal relationships, professional commitments and our own health. The nature of the disease prevents us from understanding and accepting this truth. This misunderstanding of the disease as a moral depravation issue often causes alcoholics and their family members to avoid dealing with it out of embarrassment rather than seeking help. This cycle of inaction, denial, justification and avoidance adds fuel to the fire and the results manifest themselves in unhappy families who need professional help.

Spouses and children of alcoholics usually know their alcoholic family member needs help long before the alcoholic consciously suspects it. What spouses and family members do not know is that they need help nearly as much as their alcoholic family member. So, the best course of action for the non-alcoholics in an alcoholic family becomes seeking professional counseling and attending support groups, such as Al-Anon and Al-Ateen. Even if the alcoholic family member continues to drink for years after the non-alcoholic family members seek help, the family situation will improve as those in treatment get better. They may even set an example for the alcoholic to follow that will lead to him/her doing something positive about the disease. In most cases, this does not happen until the alcoholic has a tremendously difficult situation arise from which he/she cannot deflect the blame and which is obviously caused by alcohol abuse. We alcoholics call such events "hitting bottom" and each of our "bottoms" seems different from others' "bottoms," but nearly every recovering alcoholic did not seek help until a great danger confronted him/her. Sometimes those dangers involved near death experiences, such as an automobile accident or a seizure brought on by withdrawal from alcohol. Other times, they involve an emotional danger, such as the threat of divorce or the total rejection of a child.

Loss of employment, arrest and other interventions sometimes get the alcoholic's attention, but often all of the examples I listed above do not sufficiently shake the alcoholic into action. We often have become so delusional through drinking excessively that through losing families, jobs, etc. we still drink.

Family members should never place themselves in danger by staying with or ignoring the potential dangers of an alcoholic family member. Confrontation usually does not work either. I suggest that acquiring some literature on the disease of alcoholism and recovery and placing it where the alcoholic might read it without thinking the non-alcoholic family members have intervened might help. In my drunken days, I felt hopeless of ever getting through life without alcohol and discovering that many alcoholics have successfully stopped drinking provided a ray of hope. Also, if the non-alcoholic family members know a recovering alcoholic, contacting that person might set the ball rolling in the right direction for the practicing alcoholic. In many cases, recovering alcoholics who have experienced the same hell that practicing alcoholics are currently experiencing, can reach the sick person when nobody else can.

The secret to recovery is actually simple. The practicing alcoholic must want help before any treatment can begin to succeed. Without total commitment, the practicing alcoholic will almost certainly fail. For many of us, "hitting bottom" means total hopelessness, regardless of how many material, personal or social assets we have lost because of drinking. Only when the feeling of total hopelessness takes hold can the alcoholic begin to fathom changing. Only then does it appear that a choice manifests itself and that choice is a grim one. We can either die lonely and miserably or change our lives and live. Alcohol has taken us to this point and for those of us who manage to choose to live, we face a tremendous challenge: getting totally honest with ourselves. Once we begin to do that, we can begin to heal. Once we realize that alcohol has taken so much from us and will certainly kill us if we keep on drinking, we reach the conclusion that we can never drink safely again. This realization raises another challenge: how to live and face life without alcohol. For non-alcoholics, this challenge never arises and is incomprehensible to them. For alcoholics, this challenge defines their existence, like anyone else with an unhealthy obsessive compulsive disorder.

Alcoholics use alcohol as a best friend, as an anesthetic, as a social lubricant, as a quick way to feel normal. Even if alcoholics never consciously realize that we use alcohol for all of these roles in our lives, we really do so. Smokers, who describe cigarettes as the epicenter of their lives, can substitute alcohol in alcoholics' lives and understand perfectly how important alcohol becomes to the alcoholic. People who have lost their means of coping with daily life know well what giving up alcohol is like for alcoholics. While many of us have done this many more have not managed to do so. The ease with which alcohol seemingly solves the emotional and psychological issues of life for alcoholics prevents us, in most cases, from seeing our lives as they have really become when we actively participate in our diseases. The old adage that alcoholism is a disease that tricks us into believing we have no disease rings true for alcoholics. Unfortunately, it messes up more lives than any other disease, because of the effects it has on everyone whose lives touch the lives of alcoholics.

Education is the Answer

As with so many myth-laden practices in modern society, the best solution to the problem of the alcoholic disease lies in education for everyone involved. As cigarettes have become much less fashionable than they once were, due in large part to the educational campaign waged for the past 20 plus years, that explains the health dangers and other negative consequences of smoking to all age brackets, social and ethnic groups, so such a campaign explaining alcohol and drug addiction as a disease would probably swing the pendulum in the right direction. Just as many people have taken up smoking despite the health threat and the educational campaign, many people will continue to start using and become addicted to alcohol and other mind-altering drugs. But, the effort to focus all segments of the population in the direction of correct knowledge and understanding about alcoholism as a disease will make sense almost immediately, to those who are not alcoholics, but whose lives are touched by alcoholics' lives. Also, among alcoholics who have not yet been introduced to alcohol, avoiding the initial experiment because of knowledge of the dangers involved, will doubtless reduce the numbers of users who will require treatment in the future.

As long as misled people commonly understand alcoholism as a moral problem, the problem will continue without abatement. Alcoholics and those around us will avoid seeking treatment and intervention or even discussing the problem because of guilt associated with the belief that we have a choice over whether or not to drink and fear that others will judge us morally. Of course, we really fear social alienation that often accompanies being alcoholic or a relative or associate of an alcoholic. Co-dependents will make excuses for their spouses' behaviors when drunk and children of alcoholics will avoid social contact with other people to avoid moral judgments aimed at their alcoholic parents. Maybe more importantly, the professional people who might help everyone stuck in the web of the alcoholic and drug addictions, but who are misinformed about these diseases, will continue to mis-educate people due to their own ignorance. Physicians, lawyers, counselors, educators and law enforcement officials should all have some orientation toward alcoholism and drug addiction as diseases, in order to structure their standard approaches to people with these diseases in the course of discharging their duties. Employers and other people who routinely might be affected by people suffering from these diseases should know the truth about what they face in the workplace; they face a sick person, not a criminally inclined, bum. Such sick people need help, not disciplinary action.

Of course such educational campaigns cost money and the question of who should pay for such activities becomes important, if we will launch such an educational campaign. But, I think that in the long run, the campaign will save money for society, as a whole. Reducing crime, improving productivity, improving personal relationships and the other benefits of reducing the numbers of practicing alcoholics and drug addicts interacting with people in society, will probably save money. Some programs already underway, such as DARE, designed to keep children from smoking, drinking and drugging, are helpful, but fall short of the mark in furthering the acknowledgement of alcoholism and drug addiction as diseases. Introducing this concept into the DARE Program and others, may help children of alcoholics to understand their sick parents better. Also, those children who have the addictive brain chemistry, will understand that if they have this chemical predisposition and try alcohol, they will most likely become addicted and suffer through terrible times, as well as perpetuating the cycle of addiction, abuse and emotional dysfunction that goes with practicing alcoholism.

The general public will benefit from an educational campaign, as well. For people whose lives do not closely touch the lives of alcoholics, much good can come from learning that alcoholics do not freely choose to drink to excess. For some in this category aloof from the disease, a common misperception is that alcoholics deserve ridicule and scorn, again based on the myth that alcoholism is a moral problem, not a medical problem. While the same people would scarcely laugh at an epileptic who goes into a seizure in a public place or an asthmatic, who has an attack in public, the alcoholic, equally as ill as the epileptic or asthmatic, often gets subjected to ridicule and scorn.

This erroneous double standard hinders the solution to the problem. Often children of non-alcoholics learn the same reaction of ridicule and scorn toward alcoholics from their parents. Most ironically, many alcoholics, in the early stages of the disease, ridicule and scorn other practicing alcoholics in the later stages of the same disease. Doing so often adds fuel to the denial fire in the alcoholics who have not yet begun to lose the valuable things in their lives through drinking, since, at a subconscious level, many of them know something is wrong with the way they drink alcohol, but comparing themselves to the speech-slurring, staggering and swaying, or passing out town drunk, brings temporary relief from the nagging feeling that something is wrong with their drinking behavior. I have seen this reasoning among people court-ordered to attend Alcoholics Anonymous meetings. Firmly believing the judge's decision to send them to AA is mistaken, they fail to listen to the message of those in recovery around them at the meetings. Instead, those in denial focus on the terrible exploits that most alcoholics who reach the advanced stages of the disease have taken part in, lost families, lost jobs, jail time, etc. and say to themselves, I haven't done that yet; so, I must not be an alcoholic.

Of course, the recovering alcoholics who share these horror stories at AA meetings know that their experiences with the law, with in-patient treatment facilities, with lost families, jobs, etc. came late in their drinking careers. For most of the early stages of their disease, their experiences paralleled those of the newcomers to AA who come in because they have a court order or some other outside influence. These stories reveal that the tellers know of what they speak, thereby establishing their credibility as true alcoholics, but unfortunately, the audience they intend to help often miss the point, because of denial. I remember having a completely closed mind when I first entered the rooms of Alcoholics Anonymous. I "knew" I was not an alcoholic and the fact that drinking had not cost me all of the things the "old timers" there described losing through drinking confirmed my mistaken belief that I was not an alcoholic.

I now know that these AAs attempted to save me from the terrible "yets" that, had I gotten their main points, I might have avoided. In AA meetings now, I tell my horror story, as well, but I try to make the point to the newcomers that my life was not ruined immediately from drinking and had I kept an open mind when first introduced to AA, had I thought that perhaps I was an alcoholic instead of rejecting that notion out of hand, I might have saved myself and my family a lot of problems. Unfortunately, I believe that many newcomers enter the AA rooms under the same conditions that I entered them. These newcomers attend the meetings because they have to or because of fear of losing something (job, family, freedom) if they do not demonstrate that they are trying to do something about their habitual, destructive drinking. Once the danger is removed or once their obligation to attend the meetings passes, they stop coming. In most cases, they begin the same pattern of drinking that either lands them back in AA later or, much worse, in prison, in an insane asylum or in the cemetery.

I did not learn much about alcoholism as a disease until I had entered out-patient treatment programs. In these programs, I learned that alcoholism is a disease, that it has very specific symptoms, that the disease progresses and that it will kill people if not checked. I think that these facts ought to come to light in the educational programs we all participate in at an early age. Had many of us who suffered terribly from the disease known more about the disease early in our lives, some of us would no doubt have avoided some of the trouble we got into. Also, if the families of alcoholics had learned about the symptoms and other characteristics of the disease, including its effects on them, they might have intervened earlier than they did, thus turning around a desperate situation earlier than most did so. Also, if employers and others who have occasion to associate with alcoholics realized that we are sick people, not morally depraved people, they might exercise more understanding in dealing with alcoholics, thus bringing about better consequences for everyone affected.

Understanding Solves Problems

The attitudes of the past that many people exhibited that regarded alcoholism as a morally relevant, negative, character trait, perpetuate the problems that surround the disease, as I mentioned earlier. When people confront other people in a negative or morally judgmental way, whether about alcohol or drug use and abuse, or some other subject, those confronted tend to become defensive and perhaps aggressively defensive. The phenomenon of denial emerges most frequently in scenes such as these; most alcoholics subconsciously know something is wrong with the amounts and frequency of their alcohol consumption, but to defend the delusion that we can control this inanimate substance (rather than admitting it controls us), most of us go through an extensive period of rationalizing, minimalizing, deflecting blame, and other delusional behavior to defend our behavior. Perhaps the more important motive in denial is to protect our source of euphoria.

Whatever the proximate cause of this behavior, alcoholics in denial behave in ugly, socially disgusting ways. We lie to those we love; we sometimes steal money from them to get more alcohol, and we cheat people we don't even know in pursuit of the feeling of euphoria. These actions lead to retaliation and rejection on the parts of those we hurt while we pursue our "highs." Sadly, most alcoholics do not even realize that we have done the things that cause the retaliation and rejection, because we usually have either performed these actions in alcohol-induced blackouts or under the influence of heavy drinking, so that we cannot fully bring to bear our powers of reasoning.

Non-alcoholics, who have infrequently or never experienced the complete lack of judgment and rational thought-process, that practicing alcoholics experience a good deal of the time, find it difficult to accept that the person who has just verbally abused them, lied to them, cheated them or stolen from them did not do so intentionally. The tendency to judge others based on our own experiences takes over and non-alcoholics incorrectly judge alcoholics to have acted from malicious motives, intentionally trying to hurt the victim. In truth, alcoholics rarely try to hurt anyone nor do we bear malice toward anyone. We simply instinctively protect our ability to get the feeling we crave. We correctly, though usually unconsciously, assess that non-alcoholics have no idea how we feel. We incorrectly believe that they attack us for little or not reason, when, in reality, we have hurt them first.[19]

Strangely, I believe that non-alcoholics, if properly informed, can better understand the situation that alcoholism creates for everyone affected by the disease than practicing alcoholics can. We alcoholics, when practicing, live in a foggy world where any type of high order mental activity is nearly impossible. Relatively simple issues "baffle us," as *Alcoholics Anonymous* describes our daily condition.[20] Because no medication can clear our brains from the alcohol-induced fog, we go through extended periods of time in confusion and to attempt to get a practicing alcoholic to see the reality of his/her situation while influenced by alcohol to any degree is probably impossible. Non-alcoholics, though, if capable of approaching the situation with an open mind, can more easily see that the alcoholic person, suffering from a disease over which he/she has no control, needs an understanding approach to solve the problem, both for the alcoholic and for those whose lives touch the alcoholic's life.

Putting this idea into action requires some thought and probably the advice of a professional mental health expert to insure the best chance of success on the part of the non-alcoholic. However, another approach that has a good chance of working is for the non-alcoholic to approach a recovering alcoholic, who not only can approach a practicing alcoholic on his/her level, but can advise non-alcoholics on the best methods for them to use to work with practicing alcoholics as they make an attempt at recovering. Since alcoholics are truly sick people, approaching them as we would a diabetic or hypertensive who is in denial about their conditions, promises a better outcome than confronting the alcoholics as if they chose their affliction. Clearly, nobody in their right mind would choose to live the lives that practicing alcoholics, in the advanced stages of that disease, live. Together, we can make progress toward recovery if the non-alcoholic people involved do not preach, degrade, deride or otherwise hurt the sick alcoholic.

Similarly, law enforcement personnel at all levels, employers, and other professional people whose lives cross paths with practicing alcoholics can make a positive difference through the use of understanding of alcoholism as a disease and the alcoholic as a sick person, rather than approaching us as moral deviates. I heard a story about an alcoholic who had caused an automobile accident, while drunk that injured the occupants of the other car, as well as himself. The Emergency Medical Personnel who responded to the 911 call, expressed satisfaction at his complaint of pain when they tightened the straps of the stretcher around him, because he caused the accident and he was drunk. Through their ignorance of the fact that alcoholism is a disease that does not permit him to choose between getting drunk and not getting drunk, these medical personnel perpetuate this harmful myth. If the driver of the car who caused the accident had suffered an epileptic or diabetic seizure, the EMS personnel probably would not have reacted toward him in the same way they did toward the alcoholic who was drunk.

A member of AA, for whom I have developed a great deal of respect, puts this point very succinctly. Alcoholics, who regularly attend AA meetings in the hope of staying sober, act contrary to the nature of alcoholics. By our physical nature, we drink alcohol to feel normal and staying away from it, as we do in AA, violates our most basic natural instinct. Unfortunately, many more alcoholics practice drinking than practice sobriety. Going to places to meet groups of people whose intent is to stay away from alcohol and make positive changes in their lives goes against the very nature of alcoholic people and often prevents us from getting help for a long time after we need it badly. Therefore, non-alcoholics who make moral judgments about practicing alcoholics do so out of misinformation. Though the automobile accident is tragic for all concerned, the drunk who caused it is a sick person doing what comes as naturally to him as a non-alcoholic diabetic who does not realize he has that disease. Treatment of the disease stands a better chance of solving the problem than legal action against the drunk driver.

Employers of alcoholics and addicts also should consider that if those same employees became incapacitated through some other illness, such as cancer, that employee would receive the benefit of short or long term disability and would return to the job when the incapacitation has been removed. Similarly, alcoholics and addicts are sick people who need treatment and deserve the opportunity to get better and return to work. In the long run, this course of action often benefits the business, as well, because it precludes the need to train new employees who will require long periods of time to produce on the level of a long term employee, temporarily incapacitated by alcoholism or addiction.

Across the spectrum of people affected by alcoholism and addiction, understanding and cooperation result in much more positive consequences than negative moral judgments and punitive actions. Though the numbers of recovering alcoholics, in relationship to practicing alcoholics, remains low, the increasing numbers of alcoholics in AA and in treatment programs indicate that recent efforts at understanding and education are working. The last edition of *Alcoholics Anonymous* cites the membership numbers for the organization of the same name at over the 2,000,000 mark world-wide.[21] Since 1935, when the first vestiges of AA appeared, the growth of AA has been remarkable. Much remains to be done, but by fostering understanding and passing out correct information about alcoholism as a disease and not as a moral deficiency, we move in the right direction.

VI
Implications for the Future

The Law

As a Professor of Philosophy, I have often heard that today's philosophy is next century's common sense. As this has often been the case in the past, it seems to me that we can ensure that we continue to move in the right direction, if we base moral judgments on modern knowledge and not on past myths that bred fear, contempt, anger and hostility. As laws should reflect good moral judgment, I believe we should look to reviewing current laws, as they apply to alcoholics and addicts, and revise, as needed, to protect the rights of everyone affected by these diseases. As I mentioned earlier, some laws have changed based on enlightened views of alcoholism and addiction, while others have changed, seemingly on the basis of archaic views of these conditions.

For people who commit crimes under the influence of alcohol and drugs, but who do not suffer from the diseases of alcoholism and addiction, certain moral judgments apply. However, I believe that nobody under the influence of mind-altering substances can make free choices of will regarding their actions and therefore, should not fall under the category of morally relevant judgments. For non-alcoholics and non-addicts who repeatedly commit crimes under the influence, the moral judgment that applies has to do with the choice to continue to drink or use knowing that past intoxication has led to criminal activity. The moral judgment becomes one of criminal negligence, in these cases, rather than criminal intent. But, for alcoholics and addicts, who while practicing, have neither the freedom of will to choose the actions they perform nor whether or not to drink or use, no moral judgment applies. Rather a medical judgment applies and that judgment should apply with the full force of the knowledge that left to their own devices, alcoholics and addicts will continue to drink and use and perform the actions that these substances induce them to commit. While we do not usually force people to submit to medical treatment against their wills, given the unique consequences of alcoholism and addiction to society, I believe that these cases warrant such forced medical treatment.

Also, I believe that other preventive measures that do not cost as much as court costs would lead to reduced instances of alcoholics and addicts operating cars and machinery that endanger the general public. Breath analyzers that prohibit starting cars when they detect alcohol come to mind and other such devices can help to prevent the tragedies that often result from practicing alcoholics' and addicts' actions. While no measure will entirely eliminate the problems, I believe these measures will result in at least the same measure of prevention as legal measures, if not a better success rate, at a lower cost to society.

Forced medical treatment presents a unique challenge in the cases of alcoholics and addicts who often undergo these procedures several times before they admit to themselves that they cannot control their addictions. Though many treatment programs seemingly have high failure rates, as demonstrated by the numbers of patients who have undergone in-patient and out-patient treatment more than once, every day that an alcoholic or addict is inside a treatment facility, that potential drunk driver stays off the road and lives soberly. To achieve the goal of habitual sobriety, stringing together a month of sober days potentially starts the ball rolling in the right direction. I went to in-patient treatment twice and not until the second session did I fully realize that I had to change my life or die. But, I did not waste the first session, as much of what I learned there came back to me when I needed help again later on. During both of these times, I did not drink and every day sober for alcoholics is a miracle, both for the alcoholics and for society.

Laws that allow clearly prejudicial practices that target alcoholics and addicts should likewise come under scrutiny and change, if applicable. Civil rights legislation protects the aged from discrimination based on age, protects everyone from racial, gender and national origin discrimination, because none of us have a choice over how old we are, what our skin color is nor what gender we are. Similarly, alcoholics and addicts do not choose to have these diseases and therefore, should have protection under the Civil Rights legislation, too. Termination of employment, disqualifying candidates for life and other types of insurance, and prosecution for crimes that defendants have no conscious memory of committing (let alone having no intention of committing) come to mind as practices that many legal systems support based on the archaic idea that alcoholics and addicts make free choices about their actions or about drinking and using. At worst, the legal judgment should be failure to seek proper treatment and that should only come after someone in authority has directly pointed out to the alcoholic or addict that he/she needs treatment.

The emotional appeal of such groups as Mothers Against Drunk Drivers has strongly influenced legal penalties and harsh judgments against alcoholics and addicts, in my opinion. As a parent, I also want to protect my children from all forms of danger to the greatest degree possible. I do not advocate keeping drunk or high drivers on the roads to threaten children or other innocent people's lives; however, I appeal to legal authorities at all levels to apply the logical thought processes on which our laws and their enforcement should rest to protect everyone's rights. Drunks on the road endanger their own lives as much as everyone else's lives; but, a common moral judgment and legal judgment that gets applied to them is that they are guilty of criminal activity when they are actually suffering from a serious disease. As I mentioned earlier, the judgments of non-alcoholics and addicts that people can choose not to drink or use drugs is based on the misconception that alcoholics and addicts have the same brain chemistry as non-alcoholics and non-addicts. Medical science has shown this to be false and therefore, laws should reflect this knowledge.

Common Attitudes

In the information age, knowledge of all types reaches unprecedented numbers of people through the tremendous power of the internet, satellite and cable television and other media. As these media have attacked ignorance and misunderstanding about a variety of issues facing today's society, like the obesity epidemic, domestic violence, and indebtedness, among many others, I believe that attacking the myths surrounding addictive diseases in the same manner can make a difference in the common attitudes toward these issues. Fear and misunderstanding do not solve problems; knowledge and understanding do. By educating the public about the nature of the diseases of alcoholism and drug addiction, I believe we can make much more progress in solving the problems caused by these diseases and reduce the instances of suffering alcoholics and addicts who remain untreated.

Co-dependent spouses and innocent children whose lives intimately touch the lives of victims of these diseases will gain unprecedented understanding of what's going on with the alcoholic or addict in their lives and of how these diseases adversely affect their own lives. A number of co-dependent spouses have told me that through educational programs they learned that they were sicker than their alcoholic or addict spouses. Recognizing this and knowing that help exists for them has positively changed their lives for the better. As thing stand now, only after someone intervenes directly in their lives or the lives of the alcoholics or addicts, do they receive the educational information. Before this happens many co-dependents and children feel hopeless. They perceive they have no way out of the terrible situation they did nothing to create. The tremendous feeling of hope that relieves the hopelessness can reach many more people by actively educating the general public about the diseases.

Because many co-dependents and their children feel embarrassed or somehow guilty for the behavior of their alcoholic or addicted family members, talking about the subject becomes a taboo. Rather than confront the sick person or intervene in a positive way, they skirt the subject until they cannot possibly hide it any more. As with most diseases, the earlier treatment enters into the cycle of the disease, the easier it is to arrest the disease and the fewer negative consequences suffered by everyone involved. Like attitudes toward smoking have changed because of educational programs for all ages, similar programs of education for alcoholism and drug addiction should change the attitudes people commonly hold toward these conditions. Even people whose lives have not had adverse consequences due to alcoholism or addiction might take action to help suffering alcoholics and addicts if they understand that medical procedures can arrest these diseases. But, certainly those whose lives directly touch the lives of alcoholics and addicts will benefit greatly by direct education about the diseases.

Action absorbs anxiety. This maxim has stayed with me from the first time I heard it spoken many years ago. In the cases of people who deal with practicing alcoholics and addicts on a regular basis, this maxim applies very well. The constant worry about what an alcoholic or addict in the family will do next adversely affects stability. This instability does not stop with the families of alcoholics and addicts. If people in general realize that fearing alcoholics and addicts and avoiding dealing with their conditions adds to the anxiety that this instability creates, then they may take action. The appropriate action varies in each case, but we call doing something to stem the tide of practicing alcoholism and drug addiction, intervention. Most commonly, intervention takes the form of confrontation, such as making an appointment with a professional or refusing to participate in enabling behavior. Refusing to call to make excuses for a drunk who cannot keep an important appointment because he/she is drunk is a good intervention. Many other such actions may jog the alcoholics or addicts into action themselves, though usually, it takes several such interventions to make a real difference in the behavior of the alcoholic or addict. When interventions fail to work the first time around, some family members give up on the idea and revert back to enabling patterns of behavior, but such behaviors compound the problem and lengthen the time it takes to correct the problem. Keep intervening until the alcoholic or addict cannot fail to seek help. The truth lies with the intervener and eventually, the truth will win out.

In AA, I have heard that the truth will set you free. This sentence means much in many things in life, but to the alcoholic or addict and the people whose lives are affected by these diseases, the meaning is especially important. The delusions that accompany the disease, both on the parts of the alcoholics and addicts and the co-dependents and families, create the malignant feelings that grow in all those affected. We know something is not right, but we enable ourselves to ignore the obvious. The longer this goes on, the worse the pain experienced by all. Facing the truth, though difficult, will start all involved on an incredible journey toward recovery and normalcy that most of us so afflicted appreciate more than those who have never lost touch with reality. Facing reality and working the other steps in the 12 step process of recovery become the road map to a new, much better life than anything most of us have experience before in life.

If everyone involved in the lives of alcoholics and addicts adopts the attitude of helping a sick person get better rather than enabling the delusions to continue, the recovery process can proceed more efficiently than if some continue to approach the problem as a weakness of will or a taboo situation to avoid discussing. Alcoholism is baffling for alcoholics and those around them only if we remain uneducated about the disease or refuse to accept the truth about the disease. When all or most of us understand what we deal with, the recovery moves along smoothly. We also should understand that as of now, medical professionals cannot cure alcoholism. Together, we can arrest the disease and the victims can lead very normal lives without alcohol, but the alcoholic in recovery is still an alcoholic and cannot safely take any amount of alcohol at any time. The disease progresses whether or not we drink, so that even after months or years of not drinking, the alcoholic who drinks again will shortly return to the old behavior. I falsely believed that the abstinence I experienced on several occasions would allow me to return to the days when as a teenager, I could control my drinking without getting drunk and then in trouble. Those days are long gone forever. This situation applies to every real alcoholic and addict, as *Alcoholics Anonymous*, correctly points out, "Once a drunk, always a drunk."[22] The recovery process then must become a "rest of the life" process, like a person who suffers from essential hypertension (high blood pressure), who must take medication for the rest of his life or else risk the consequences of elevated blood pressure or the diabetic, who also faces an incurable, but arrestable, disease.

New and Old Treatments

In the course of time that I drank and made half-hearted efforts to get help, because I wanted to get out of trouble with the people around me, I saw several psychiatrists. I learned from them that nowhere in the annals of mental health developments or in physical health breakthroughs has anyone discovered a new treatment for alcoholism that promises to make the alcoholic's recovery easy. All of them told me they offered me little hope; the only hope lay in the 12 steps of Alcoholics Anonymous. As I saw the psychiatrists only because I had to in order to keep up the appearance of trying to stop drinking, I paid little attention to what they told me. With the benefit now of several years of sobriety and that mostly coming as a result of Alcoholics Anonymous, I know clearly what the psychiatrists meant. A bit disconcerting for these learned men and women perhaps, but AA has accomplished for over 2 million alcoholics what all the science so far applied to the problem has failed to accomplish. We of AA have hope, for many of us, for the first times in our lives. The AA program is simple, but it's not easy and without becoming totally honest with ourselves, it has proven to be impossible for many of us. I will spend more time on the program a little later, but to address any treatment for addictive disease without the 12 step program of recovery would be to leave out the only proven solution over any considerable time period.

Having plugged the AA program, I also know that medical and mental health professionals have made significant progress in addressing some of the common physical problems associated with practicing alcoholism and addiction and have used a very good mental health approach that has no doubt contributed significantly to many of our recoveries. The human body has amazed many people who have studied it over the years and, perhaps one of the more amazing capabilities lies in how quickly it can begin to rebuild all of its parts that long term alcohol poisoning have damaged. The liver, for example, can rejuvenate itself amazingly quickly once alcohol no longer flows through it.   But, for me, the most amazing part of alcoholism treatment lays in the results of group psychotherapy. The counselors with whom I worked managed to identify in my past those episodes that led to the hidden demons that I had no clue were inside me. Through their efforts, I came to grips with a number of events in my past life over which I had never had closure and which, when I confronted them, disappeared as emotional issues for me. I discovered that I had hidden a great deal of guilt, fear and resentment inside me and covered these negative feelings with alcohol to the extent that I did not know I had these demons. Through the psychotherapy, I emerged a free man and through working the 12 steps of AA, I remain a free man.

In days past, physicians and psychiatrists who specialized in the treatment of alcoholism experienced a great deal of discouragement due to misunderstanding on everyone's part about the nature of the disease. In the 1930s, treatments centered around hospitalization for some weeks, during which abstinence from alcohol and drugs settled the alcoholic down and treated some of the physical maladies that often accompany alcohol abuse, such as dehydration, malnutrition, nervousness and anxiety. But, as Dr. Silkworth, the physician who wrote prefacing letters for the first two editions of *Alcoholics Anonymous*, admitted, the work did not reward the medical professionals well, because they rarely succeeded in keeping alcoholics sober for extended periods of time.[23] Also, given the unique denial symptoms of addictive diseases that the earlier medical personnel did not understand, the alcoholics and addicts who came to hospitals for treatment did not receive a warm welcome. Knowing that the patients would lie to them, the physicians found it nearly impossible to learn accurate case histories of the patients and therefore, could not apply the rudimentary treatments effectively.

We alcoholics, when practicing, still lie to everyone concerning the amounts and frequencies of alcohol consumption, believing that we fool the people who question us. This terribly ironic truth lends credence to the theory that we suffer from obsessive/compulsive behavior where alcohol is concerned, because in many cases, our actual lives depend on accurately answering the physicians' questions. Still, we lie, in hopes that we can get away to drink another day, taking chances with our health and lives that can only fall into the category of obsessive/compulsive behavior. With everything to lose, the craving to continue drinking blots out reality and we do the most irrational things we could do under the circumstances. As the authors of *Alcoholics Anonymous* point out, many medical people, physical and mental health experts, think lowly of practicing alcoholics, because we routinely lie to them.[24]

Modern specialists in alcoholism and addiction realize that these lies do not fall into the category of intentional lies, in the same sense that non-alcoholics and non-addicts lie to other people. One symptom of these diseases is lying to protect one's ability to continue the destructive behavior. Knowing this in advance, modern medical specialists in alcoholism treatment put little credence in what alcoholics tell them about how much and how often they drink. Though some differences in treatment exist for people in different stages of the disease, those in the most advanced stage have physical symptoms that tell the true story of their drinking histories and patterns, so physicians can properly prescribe the treatment. Perhaps as important, physicians now realize that alcoholics and addicts who lie about their drinking and using behaviors are not morally culpable for these lies. In many cases, the alcoholics and addicts believe the lies they tell; they suffer from delusional behavior. The physicians therefore can approach treatment more rationally without mistakenly believing the moral worst about their patients.

Some drugs have mixed success in keeping alcoholics from drinking in the difficult early days of sobriety. Though producing different affects on people who drink while these drugs are in their systems, the idea that either negating the euphoria alcohol produces or inducing violent nausea and allergic reactions, will prevent the alcoholic from drinking while taking these drugs sometimes works and often does not. Many of us have endured worse sickness in withdrawal or because of overdosing on alcohol than the illness producing drug creates. Also, even the reduced euphoria caused by the other drug feels better to many alcoholics than no euphoria at all, and some of us drink despite taking these medications. For those for whom these drugs work, the results are sometimes good. For some of us, staying away from the drug of choice for a period of weeks or months, gives us the opportunity to make the attitude changes needed to recover fully. Each case is somewhat different from the next.

Recent research has led to a number of theoretical drug treatments that have some hope of eliminating the craving for alcohol in alcoholics. Such a drug, if reliable and safe, would revolutionize the treatment of this terrible disease, save lives and greatly improve the quality of life for the many alcoholics who suffer from the disease and the people whose lives come into close contact with the alcoholic. How far into the future such drug treatment may lie, nobody knows for certain. As for now, the real hope for alcoholics and their families and associates lies in a combination of the therapies mentioned above.

In my case, I needed the abstinence that the drugs helped enforce, coupled with the intense group psychotherapy and education that in-patient treatment afforded me. After leaving in-patient treatment, I needed the weekly aftercare psychotherapy sessions to continue to bolster the tools I learned in in-patient treatment to stay sober. Most importantly for me, I needed to regularly attend AA meetings, work the 12 steps of the recovery process and help other alcoholics, as time went on. The point of the AA program centers on the biggest problem for me, how to live life without alcohol after relying on alcohol for many years to fill so many emotional and psychological roles in my life. By voluntarily adopting the AA program, I have become a free man: free from the compulsion to drink alcohol. I continue to work the steps every day in hopes of becoming a little better each day. I have come a little way in emotional and spiritual development from where I started in the AA program and I have a long way to go. Ironically, I love the idea that I will have something to work on (spiritual progress) for the rest of my life. Every day offers me a new challenge concerning what I can do to improve a little from yesterday. Since adopting this new way of life, I have not felt the need to take a drink. I sometimes think about drinking, but never in the way I used to and I don't obsess about where I will get my next drink, how I will deceive people about my drinking and how I will cover up the destructive consequences of my drinking. I do not feel guilt, fear, anxiety or stress over these (or anything else) any more. I am free.

Today's Climate of Acceptance

To keep the record straight, I think I should acknowledge that in the past 25 to 30 years, many more people than previously have adopted an acceptance of alcoholism as a disease and of the alcoholic as a sick person. Largely the results, in my opinion, of highly regarded people coming forward to acknowledge that they have the disease, have sought treatment, and have moved into a program of recovery for life, this new acceptance is only a beginning. More people than not still regard alcoholism as a moral defect that should result in punishment of some kind, either legal or social punishment, but not medical treatment. To alleviate the negative effects of this type of reasoning, I propose that all of us who have the benefit of knowledge of the disease, its symptoms and its treatment must do more than we have in the past. Physicians who have special training in the alcoholic disease should pass on to other physicians who do not have the same specialized training the benefit of the correct knowledge. Legal people who have knowledge of the alcoholic disease should likewise educate legal professionals who do not have that knowledge. Employers who know that alcoholism is a disease should attempt to educate the workforce about this news. Families who have experienced the ravages of alcoholism and recovered together with the alcoholic family member should reach out to other families who still suffer from this disease's dysfunctions. Everyone involved can make a difference.

Armed with facts about the disease and about people who have the disease and recovered to make significant contributions to society will help everyone to pass on accurate information. Alcoholics have a deficiency in certain brain chemicals that cause them to become addicted when alcohol is introduced into their systems. Addiction to alcohol produces a craving that alcoholics cannot resist, except under the greatest pressure, and that eventually causes the alcoholic to give in to alcohol abuse regardless of the consequences. The greatest desire to stop drinking cannot help an alcoholic unless he/she receives some professional help. The alcoholics' actions while drunk negatively affect everyone whose life touches the alcoholics' lives, especially family members and others who have a loving relationship with alcoholics. Current treatment methods offer the opportunity to arrest the disease through abstinence from alcohol, but not a cure. As of now, once an alcoholic, always an alcoholic. Family members can also recover from the affects of living with an alcoholic over extended periods of time, doing much the same things that a recovering alcoholic does. In the end, many of us recover to practice medicine, mental health, law, education, business management and all other worthy professions and careers.

This short summary truly captures the essence of what an accepting attitude toward alcoholism can mean. To adopt the more common and archaic attitude toward alcoholism as a moral deficiency is to doom most efforts at recovery to failure or at least to delay the recovery needlessly. The next consideration should lie in the specific actions each of us might take if we find ourselves in a position to help an alcoholic who still suffers.

The Family Approach to Treatment

Catastrophic diseases affect not only the disease victims, but those who have emotional, physical and psychological ties to the victim. But, no disease affects everyone around the victim in the ways that alcoholism and drug addiction affect the families, employers, co-workers, friends, associates and health care providers involved. Family members usually become victims of their own syndromes as a result of long term exposure to an alcoholic family member. Employers become embittered and resentful of their sick employees; long time friends feel betrayed, and health care professionals feel discouraged because of the difficulties involved in helping alcoholics and addicts to recover.

Families, more than any other category, suffer uniquely from their ordeals. Mainly because they believe the myths that perpetuate through generations about alcoholism as a moral deficiency and also, because alcoholics usually place the blame for their excessive drinking on the family members, families often come out of these affairs more ill than the alcoholic. I also have personal experience with the syndrome called, "The Adult Child of an Alcoholic." My father was an alcoholic, who refused to accept this truth, mostly out of ignorance of what alcoholism is. Nonetheless, he drank alcoholically when he drank and, more importantly, he behaved like an alcoholic, selfishly and emotionally hollow. The results of having an emotionally absent parent on children manifest themselves in a number of ways. The inability of my father to show emotions that characterizes alcoholic parents had a profound effect on me. I pray that I have somewhat broken that cycle with my children, but I certainly removed myself emotionally from my children when I drank.

The spouses of alcoholics also suffer terribly in this disease. As the person they knew, loved and married changes markedly over time, the spouses change, as well. Guilt, fear and resentment build up inside them and they withdraw emotionally from their alcoholic spouse, as well as withdrawing socially from the community, as a result of these same negative emotions. *Alcoholics Anonymous* describes the affects of long term alcoholism on a family in an analogy to a tornado that has destroyed every possession of family except the clothing on their backs.[25] If the alcoholic is blessed enough to enter recovery, he/she usually emerges from the fray with a positive attitude, suddenly realizing how close to death he/she had come. Without realizing how much damage our drinking caused to our family members, we become immediately thankful and positive in outlook, while our families remain in the ruins of sprees.

For this reason, modern treatment often emphasizes the need for families to heal together. In many in-patient treatment programs, spouses spend some of the time with their alcoholic spouses in an attempt to start the process moving for both members. Unfortunately, many non-alcoholic spouses of alcoholics do not think they have problems that will not disappear when the alcoholic stops drinking. Therefore, in many cases, the non-alcoholic spouse remains emotionally and psychologically ill while the alcoholic gets better. After years, in many cases, of emotional absence, if not abuse, the non-alcoholic spouse needs therapy as much as the alcoholic does. In some cases, marriages that survived the active drinking break up when the alcoholic gets sober, because the non-alcoholic spouse does not know how to deal with the newly sober person in his/her life. Also, some marriages took place while the alcoholic was drinking and after sobriety, the couple discovers that they really had little or nothing in common when alcohol gets removed from the equation.

The failure of non-alcoholic spouses and children of alcoholics to seek treatment coincidentally with the alcoholic's treatment or shortly thereafter, sometimes contributes to the further alienation of the alcoholic from the family and eventually to a complete breakup. At best, such a situation delays for extended time periods the benefits of family healing. By going through a crisis together and surviving that crisis together, personal relationships get stronger. But when the recovery centers only on one member, i.e. the alcoholic, the family health continues to suffer. Non-alcoholic spouses and children who do not get help often resent that the alcoholic gets better physically, mentally and emotionally, while they continue to feel the self-pity, fear, guilt and other negative emotions that active alcoholism has caused. Therefore, educating everyone concerned about the typical effects of this disease on the family at the beginning of the alcoholic's treatment is imperative.

Aside from individual counseling for the family members and group therapy, the support groups, such as Al-Anon and Al-Ateen, provide invaluable benefits to the families. For many, the discovery that other people have experienced the same calamities that they have faced and survived is a tremendous blessing in itself. Also, the healing process that comes of the freedom to share feelings and listen to others who have weathered similar storms has manifested itself in many family members of alcoholics. If everyone in the family seeks help at the same time, the family will realize the maximum benefit in the shortest time possible. Often the families experience the same type of denial as the alcoholic demonstrates as a symptom of the disease. This denial prevents them from finding relief from the ravages of having an alcoholic in the family and their denial usually comes from the same source as the alcoholic's denial, belief in the myths associated with alcoholism over the years. Not willing to admit to a family member's moral deficiency and the stigma attached to that judgment, they deny that anything is wrong, when they know inside there is something terribly wrong.

What Employers Should Do

Leaders and managers have difficult jobs when issues like alcoholism do not present themselves for resolution in the workplace. When such issues arise, the challenges for managers become exponentially greater. Unfortunately, most training sessions for managers do not include the most effective and logical set of choices for dealing with alcoholism in the workplace. Based largely on the myths of choice and moral deficiency, the tools that managers have to use will largely fail to solve the problem for either the employer or the alcoholic employee, as these tools fall into the category of punitive measures, designed to frighten the alcoholic into not drinking in order to avoid punishment. In many cases, good employees, who also happen to suffer from alcoholism, have lost their jobs due to the misunderstanding on the parts of their employers about alcoholism as a disease. As I mentioned earlier, especially in advanced cases of alcoholism, threats do not work. Alcoholics cannot just stop drinking like non-alcoholics can easily do. Even the strongest desire to stop drinking cannot keep an alcoholic deeply into the disease from drinking. The alcoholic needs immediate help from medical professionals in such cases.

Compounding the issues surrounding alcoholism in the workplace is the denial that alcoholics, even in the final stages of the disease, exhibit. Employers sometimes take the failure of their threats of punishment and termination on the parts of alcoholic employees as indications of insubordination or apathy. In reality, alcoholics cannot admit to themselves that they have the alcoholic disease and, with impaired judgment due to heavy drinking, none of the traditional methods employers typically use to handle alcoholics in the workplace work to either party's satisfaction. The delusion that we can still control how much we drink or stop altogether whenever we want remains with alcoholics until we have proper intervention. This clearly irrational posture sometimes causes employers to become angry and to make emotional decisions based on erroneous beliefs. Nothing drunks do when under the influence of alcohol accurately reflects what we would do if not under the influence. In fact, employment problems would most likely not exist at all, if alcohol did not enter the picture.

As sick people, alcoholics should receive serious treatment before employers terminate their employment or punish them for actions performed while under the influence. Like employees suffering from other diseases, alcoholics need help to try to get better and to continue our employment while in treatment is the only logical course of action, if we believe we should not terminate employees who have other diseases. Often the normal length of treatment for alcoholism in in-patient facilities is insufficient for alcoholics in deep denial to fully comprehend our situation. On completion of these treatments, alcoholics still in denial often relapse, going on to another drinking spree. In these cases, I suggest each employer must decide on the merits of other considerations whether or not the alcoholic employees are worth a second chance at treatment. But, as with some forms of cancer and other diseases, relapses commonly occur with alcoholism and accurately predicting success or failure of treatment for these cases becomes very difficult. I do not suggest that employers have a duty to continue to employ alcoholics who have repeatedly attended treatment and repeatedly failed. But, at some point, such treatment usually succeeds and these employees will almost certainly perform at levels beyond any we attained prior to becoming sober. By applying a non-confrontational approach and an enlightened understanding of the disease, employers will usually communicate effectively with alcoholic employees. However, more traditional approaches include confrontational attitudes and threatening behavior that shut off effective communications and often doom the initial attempt to help to failure from the start.

Enlightenment for Everyone

I have covered suggestions for the most commonly affected non-alcoholic people to deal with alcoholics in their lives. Many other possible relationships between non-alcoholics and alcoholics exist, but for everyone who has the potential to have to deal with a practicing alcoholic, acceptance of alcoholism as a disease and assuming an understanding attitude will almost always help in solving the problem rather than making it worse. Many non-alcoholics not only misunderstand alcoholism as a disease, but fear practicing alcoholics as dangerous people to be around. Mostly, we do not pose a direct danger to others in a physical sense, unless while driving or when in possession of a weapon of some sort. But, face to face, a drunk usually has very poor balance, little hand-eye coordination and little strength due to the toxic effects of alcohol.

The fear of the unknown and misunderstood also affects the reactions of non-alcoholics when confronted by drunks. By learning of alcoholism as a disease and recognizing the need for treatment, non-alcoholics can perhaps save a life, by intervening in the lives of practicing alcoholics. Often, non-alcoholics avoid contact with alcoholics or report drunken behavior to the police. As things stand now, in many cases, the police arrest the impaired persons and then release them once they have sobered up. A small fine usually results from the charges of drunk in public, but nothing gets resolved. The alcoholic will most likely get drunk again at the first opportunity. If the alcoholics, in these cases, went to hospitals or other treatment facilities, rather than jail, they might start on the road to recovery. Going to jail in these cases solves no problem. By treating the alcoholic as a criminal, rather than a sick person, the problem of alcoholism in these people perpetuates.

In similar cases involving people ill with other diseases, such as epilepsy, the public knows to call an ambulance automatically. But practicing alcoholics, every bit as ill as epileptics, usually get arrested instead of getting medical treatment. The crime of "drunk in public" makes as much sense as "epileptic in public." No epileptic chooses to have a seizure in public or in private and no alcoholic chooses to get drunk, either in public or in private. The myth of choice, in these cases, gets perpetuated by the laws in force, that do not accord at all with the medical judgments we who have lived with the illness of alcoholism and treated it have learned about it. The solutions to a number of problems lie in solving the misunderstanding and smashing the myths associated with alcoholism as a moral issue rather than a medical issue.

VII
What To Do If You Think You Have the Disease of Alcoholism

Get Honest

I believe that as a group of people, alcoholics tell lies more than most other groupings of people. Apart from our disease, alcoholics are basically like other people, some honest, some dishonest and many somewhere in between. But, when alcohol becomes a topic of discussion, specifically the amount or frequency of alcohol consumption or our behavior when under the influence of alcohol, most alcoholics become almost totally dishonest. We lie to our spouses, parents, children, employers, co-workers, friends and associates. Even more importantly, we lie to ourselves. We minimalize the amounts that we drink, rationalize why we drink and distort the truth about how much alcohol affects our lives. Medical professionals who specialize in treating alcoholics or suspected alcoholics, almost always know that we lie about how much we consume. Knowing this, these medical professionals often record double the amounts we admit to drinking when they ask us, in order to have a more realistic picture of an important piece of medical information.

When our family members ask us why we drink so often and so much, we usually have any number of excuses, like job stress, unhappiness with our lots in the workplace or home, something the person asking has done or failed to do, the need to relax, etc. All of these excuses have some believability to people not educated about the disease of alcoholism, but in truth, alcoholics drink for one reason: we are alcoholics and have an addiction to that drug. Close examination of what happens to we alcoholics as a result of our drinking proves beyond a reasonable doubt that none of the excuses we use stands up in the light of reason. We drink to get the euphoric feeling alcohol produces, even to the detriment to our health, our personal relationships, our employment, and our social connections.

Having noted that alcoholics tell more lies than most people and that we believe the worst lies ourselves, the pressing problem that faces us is how to get honest when dishonesty has become so natural to us, insofar as alcohol is concerned. First, we have to know the truth in order to accept it and perpetuate it. Most of us have no idea that we drink alcoholically, because we make uneducated assumptions about alcoholism and its symptoms. Even after years of exposure to the educational part of alcoholism treatment, I mistakenly believed my own delusion that I never set out directly to get drunk. My definition of "drunk" did not concur with the legal or medical definition of "drunk." I believed that I was drunk when my speech slurred, when I staggered when walking, when I had difficulty recognizing other people, etc. But, the correct definition of "drunk" centers on the amount of alcohol in a person's bloodstream, a level at which judgment, reflexes and thought processes slow down and become impaired. By this definition, I hardly ever drew a sober breath during my drinking days. When the blood-alcohol content equals 0.08, we are legally and medically drunk and I always exceeded that level when I drank. For people of moderate physical stature, two drinks (two 12 oz. beers, two 1.5 oz shots of hard liquor or two 8 oz glasses of wine) within an hour of consumption, puts them close to or over the legal limit. I drank that much alcohol within the first five minutes of a drinking spree that would last for hours. Indeed, I always drank to get drunk, using the correct definition of "drunk."

Most alcoholics have gotten drunk by my definition many times, but have stopped short of that degree of intoxication when other things prevented them from going to that extreme. Unfortunately, we rarely recognize that we do not really control our drinking at these times, but some other factors keep us from going on to complete obliteration. We still have gotten drunk, just not very drunk. Sometimes vague memories of drinking patterns long ago remain with us that give us the delusion that we still control our drinking. Also, few of us keep close tabs on how much we drink at any given time, so the significant increase in volume and frequency of drinking goes unnoticed by the practicing alcoholic. But usually at some time, the thought occurs to us that we have evolved in how much and how often we drink into a situation that is beyond normal. At this point, we usually dismiss the thought with a trivial excuse and continue to drink and in truth, we cannot slow down significantly or quit drinking entirely without professional help at this point in the disease. We became "hooked" much earlier in the disease progression, in the majority of cases. That we do not recognize that we are hooked often is the result of the debilitating effects of alcohol on us. Alcohol makes us feel serene when our lives are collapsing around us. The subtlety with which this happens lulls us into a sense of security and we usually ignore vivid warning signs that we are headed for disaster because of the substance that causes these terrible consequences.

At whatever point practicing alcoholics realize we are in trouble, usually when we've lost most of the most valuable things in life, the only hope for us lies in honesty. It usually takes either a professional medical person or a recovering alcoholic to get through the fog that alcohol has caused in the minds of the suffering alcoholic to start this process. Someone who will know how to sort through the "garbage" that practicing alcoholics throw out to deflect criticism and to avoid serious scrutiny of the mess our lives have become, has a much better chance of reaching the alcoholic than someone who has no idea of how strong the defenses have become that alcoholics typically build up around themselves. Some of us, on hearing that honesty is the first step to recovery, start to admit some truth about their actions when drunk to people close to them, but rarely take the needed self-evaluation without some difficulty.

The honesty required to recover starts with ourselves. We must admit, not in words, but sincerely believe, that we are alcoholics, sick people, and that alcohol has taken control of our lives. We must come to believe firmly that we can never again drink alcohol safely, i.e. without risking serious consequences, like loss of families, loss of jobs, loss of possessions, etc. That realization, not just mouthing those words, lays the foundation for everything else that we must do to recover. To get to a point where we can begin to honestly evaluate ourselves, we must have gotten all vestiges of alcohol from our systems and place ourselves somewhere where getting alcohol is difficult. Without alcohol to cloud our judgments and with the help of a recovering alcoholic, practicing alcoholics can start on the right road. We begin by examining what alcohol has cost us in our lives. We continue by examining the delusional reasons we gave ourselves for drinking at all and acknowledging that they have no basis in reality. None of the excuses make sense; we drink because we are addicted to alcohol and no other reason. Knowing that we cannot stop drinking without help and wanting to prevent the terrible consequences that almost always follow drinking episodes, we make up our minds to do whatever is necessary to get sober and stay sober. Almost immediately, we feel hope. Almost immediately, we feel relief from the guilt, resentments, fears and self-pity that have weighed us down for as long as alcohol has interfered with our living normally. Almost immediately, others begin to see a change in us. We have begun to be free people, free from a form of slavery that we could not recognize just days before, in some cases.

The honesty required to relieve the compulsion to drink comes in different degrees of difficulty depending on the individual alcoholic. But, I have never heard any recovering alcoholic say that the self-evaluation and honest realization of what we have done came easily. Regardless of the degree of difficulty, we must take this step first and we must continue to accept the truth of our disease throughout recovery, if we want to live at all normally. Many of us have thought we were taking the first step when we were not. So many ask the questions, "What do I have to do?" "How will I know that I'm taking the right steps?" I understand these questions, since I have lived through these uncertainties. I advise those who find themselves asking these questions to think about why they are asking the questions. Why do we want these answers? Do we want to appear as if we are doing something about our drinking, so that other people will stop badgering us or because an employer has threatened us with harsh consequences if we do not do something about our drinking? If the answer to why we're asking these questions is anything but, "Because I want to stop drinking for good," then we have not made an adequate self-evaluation and we have not gotten totally honest with ourselves.

The first step in the AA 12 step process for recovery reads, "We admitted we were alcoholics; that our lives had become unmanageable."[26] The words sometimes get in the way of alcoholics' recoveries, because many cannot accept the idea that our lives are unmanageable. We have jobs, families, homes, etc. We pay the bills, for the most part, on time. We often feel that because we take care of these physical necessities of life, we deserve to drink, as our reward. But, we almost always have neglected our own emotional and spiritual well-being, as well as that of our family members. We owe love and communication to our spouses and children and few of us can give that because we isolate ourselves emotionally from them when we drink. As our emotional relationships fall apart, we fail to notice because we have alcohol to fall back on. Usually, by the time someone confronts us with our drinking behavior, we have unmanageable spiritual and emotional lives. Also, our physical lives are beginning to become unmanageable. In the sense that Step 1 means it, our lives have become unmanageable.

Admitting we are alcoholics and our lives are unmanageable seems one of the hardest things for alcoholics to do. I suggest that people to whom the thought has occurred that they drink too much or that they should slow down or quit drinking should seriously open their minds to the possibility that they have the disease of alcoholism. People who do not have this disease do not have thoughts like this about drinking. Drinking does not enter their thoughts at all. If anyone has commented on another person's drinking, the persons about whom the comments were made, should open their minds to the possibility that they have the alcoholic disease. People who have had severe hangovers and continue to drink alcohol in later episodes, should open their minds to the possibility that they have the disease. People who have lied to anyone else about drinking, either how much, how often or behavior while drinking, should open their minds to the possibility they may be alcoholics. People who have hidden their drinking from others, either their employers, co-workers, family members, friends, etc., should open their minds to the possibility that they may be alcoholics.

By opening their minds these people have taken an important step toward honesty. *Alcoholics Anonymous* describes a test for people who are unsure of whether or not they are alcoholics.[27] Don't take a drink for a year. This simple test is almost impossible for alcoholics to pass, since we will almost certainly find some excuse to drink over that period of time. Another suggested test involves doing "controlled drinking," starting to drink and stopping after one or two drinks without difficulty in stopping and not going on a binge shortly after the experiment. Of the stories I have heard alcoholics tell in AA meetings, no real alcoholic can stop drinking for a year without craving a drink (wanting a drink badly) nor drink socially (controlled drinking). I remember thinking during my drinking days that I could not imagine not drinking for a year. Too many special occasions would interfere with such a plan and I did not know any other way to celebrate special occasions than drinking alcohol. That thought alone should have told me that I am an alcoholic, but I did not even consider that possibility when drinking. Also, I never went into a bar and just drank one beer or drink. Though I believed that I did not get drunk very often, since I walked out the bars and drove safely home, I know now that I was always legally drunk when I left those bars, just because of the numbers of drinks I needed to feel the euphoria.

I have provided a number of suggestions for how people can determine if they are alcoholics or not, but though I hope many will try these out and discover the truth about themselves, I have doubts that many will. We alcoholics have closed our minds to the idea that we have a problem and therefore, it usually takes a terrible loss to convince us we need help. To the degree that some of us can open our minds and at least accept the possibility that we have the alcoholic disease before we "hit bottom," I hope I can influence this process. Like any disease, the earlier the diagnosis and treatment, the better all the way around.

Change in Attitude

For those who acknowledge their disease, the recovery process revolves around honesty. Some alcoholics in early recovery have decided to start telling the truth to everyone around them about everything they can think of. While I suggest that such honesty to others is generally the best policy, sometimes it backfires because to suddenly get honest with everyone else hurts them or others. Examples include telling spouses about illicit love affairs that went on when the alcoholics were drinking, telling employers about episodes they previously did not know about on the job, etc. But, the honesty that recovery depends on is self-knowledge and self-evaluation:

honesty about ourselves. Once we get honest with ourselves about our alcoholism, the next step involves changing our attitudes.

Alcohol as a drug serves as a depressant. Though the initial feeling it seems to produce feels like a stimulant, this feeling is one of the deceptive characteristics of the drug. We crave this initial feeling, but the reality of the effects of alcohol in the long run in every drinking episode is that within 20 to 30 minutes, the euphoria begins to wear off and depression of every body system begins. In this state, we usually feel sorry for ourselves because of the loss of euphoria and, in general, whether we have alcohol in our systems or not, we feel depressed for the most part. Our general outlook is selfish, while involved in the cycle of getting drunk on a repetitive basis. As *Alcoholics Anonymous* accurately describes it, alcoholics have a fundamental problem and alcohol is not it.[28] We are selfish, self-centered, delusional and prone to self-pity. If we want to get better, to recover from the symptom of drinking continuously, we must change our attitudes. We must stop the selfishness and take interest in others.

During the first week of my in-patient treatment, my counselor told me to change my attitude or leave. By this he meant to stop dwelling on how bad my life had become and become grateful for what I had. In my mind, I had lost everything worth having in life, so I could not see what I had to be grateful for. My counselor told me to start with the fact that I woke up that morning and many people who have my disease did not wake that morning. Also, I had four walls around me and a roof over my head, while many people who have my disease did not. I had access to three good meals a day and many people who have my disease did not. He told me to make two lists when I got back to my living quarters, on one side list the things in my life about which I had regrets and on the other side, list the things in my life about which I should be grateful. When I carried out this assignment, I discovered that the list of things about which to be grateful exceeded the other list by five times. I immediately began to change my attitude.

From that day on, I wake up every day and thank God for what I have. I do not lament things that do not go my way, as I have come to believe that God has taken control of my life and what I want at any given time may not be in the grand plan for my life and therefore not the best thing for me. Every day, I can look back to that day several years ago and see that my life today is much better in every way than it was when I had this awakening. Getting sober did not solve life's challenges; bad things still happen to good people. However, I deal with these issues now sober. I do not use alcohol to escape from them. As I have heard a number of recovering alcoholics say, no problem in life is so bad, that alcohol cannot make it worse. I have experienced this first hand on many occasions. Drinking always complicated further even the most challenging times in my life. Today, I can face anything sober and can usually figure out how to deal with the situation, a state of affairs that is much different from when I drank every day.

My counselor also told me to "get out of myself." It took me a while to understand what he meant, but I came to the conclusion that I had to make a conscious effort to reach out to other people. One day, shortly after I left in-patient treatment, I thought about doing something for someone else. I asked myself who that should be and immediately I thought of my wife and daughters, who I love dearly. I went to a greeting card store and bought three cards for no special occasion. I wrote on the interiors that I was thinking about them and that I loved them. I sent the cards out and amazingly to me, all of them called me to tell me how nice it was to receive the cards and to know I thought about them. A small gesture that paid big dividends.

Today, I still try to let them know every day that I think about them and in addition, I have tried to reach out to other people. For most of us in recovery, we can find a lot of people to reach out to in suffering alcoholics. We, in recovery, have much good that we can do, just by demonstrating that recovery is possible to those who still suffer from the symptoms of the disease. Another change in attitude that I found necessary for recovery is in my spiritual life. I had not prayed or attempted to contact a higher power in many years. *Alcoholics Anonymous* identifies the root of the alcoholics' problems as self-centeredness and selfishness.[29] I certainly fit that description when I drank. I believed myself entirely self-sufficient; I developed an arrogance and the false sense of invincibility that it took a long, hard fall to break. While at in-patient treatment, I realized that left to my own resources, I would get drunk again shortly after I left the facility. I had to completely give in to the idea that I could not control alcohol; alcohol controlled me. My counselors, as well as a number of AA members, told me that the only hope for me lies in developing and increasing a conscious contact with a higher power and leaving to that higher power my recovery. So, I admitted that I could not deal with alcohol, so I asked my higher power, God, to relieve me of the compulsion to drink. So far, God has complied, as long as I try to improve my life in the areas over which I can make a difference.

Every day, I pray twice, once in the morning after waking up and once in the night, just before going to sleep. Following the suggestions in the 12 steps of AA, I pray for God to remove my character defects and for knowledge of His will for me and the strength and courage to carry out that will.[30] I do not pray for good things to happen to me, like hitting the lottery, getting a promotion at work, etc. God will take care of those kinds of things if they happen to be part of His plan for me. If not, God will show me some other courses of action that will allow me to carry out His will for me. The spiritual part of the recovery program has become the most important part of my life. I feel a sense of serenity and humility that I never knew before. When events do not occur the way I would have like them to go, I now believe that God has some other plan in mind for me that will serve me better in the long run. When events go the way I want them to, I assume that my will is in sync with God's will for me on that issue. God has solved many of my problems that I otherwise would have complicated, if not completely botched.

Along with the serenity and humility that I learned and received from the 12 step recovery program, I learned to adjust my attitude toward other people. I try, though I do not always succeed, to accept other people for who they are, without criticizing them or trying to change their behavior, beliefs, or thoughts. Live and let live is one of the mottos by which recovering alcoholics usually try to live. I learned that problems often work themselves out with no intervention from me. While drinking, I would insert my will into many people's business with whom I had no right to interfere. Usually, my meddling confused things greatly without a good resolution to the issue. Now, I realize that I can only change myself and affecting the needed changes in me takes all the effort I can muster.

Seek Counseling

After numerous attempts to prove to myself that I could drink responsibly, without negative consequences, I came to realize, through disastrous results, that I could not drink without negative consequences and that I could not stop drinking without help. Among the thousands of stories of alcoholics that I have heard over the years in AA, none of them indicate any success in moderating or stopping drinking on the parts of any real alcoholics, without some outside help, either counseling, AA, or both. My experiences with the trained professionals in both out-patient and in-patient alcohol rehabilitation programs has been great. Though I did not get their messages to me for quite some time, they never gave up on me. They know alcoholism inside and out and when I finally took their advice, I got better.

Most alcoholics, aside from the chemical dependency, have emotional issues that need resolved if we hope to live with any degree of peace and contentment. Having anesthetized my feelings into oblivion for many years by getting drunk whenever a significant life-altering event passed, I had a lot of "demons" to deal with when beginning sobriety. Because I suppressed so many strong emotions for so long, my best chance of staying sober came by removing those demons from my subconscious mind and beginning to deal with them consciously while still under the care of trained professionals. I had never brought closure to events, like my parents' deaths, which the treatment program allowed me to. By starting my new life in sobriety without those demons lurking in the subconscious mind, I bought a little more insurance against relapse once the problems of life began to come around again.

I hesitated to go to both out-patient and in-patient treatment, largely because I still believed the myths associated with alcoholism. To seek counseling would amount to an admission of insanity, of weakness, to my way of thinking and I resisted such admissions with all my delusional strength. However, having participated in both programs, I now believe they offer the best initial solution for alcoholics who want to recover. I learned that the myths I believed about alcoholism were false and that the people in the programs at the same times I attended them, had a lot in common with me. Not only did we have alcohol dependence in common, but we had a number of emotional issues and spiritual bankruptcy in common. For those who developed a willingness to do whatever it took to get better, the programs generally worked. For those who did not develop that willingness, the programs usually failed. The failure did not lie in the content of the program, but in the patients who could not accept the fact that they are fatally ill and could not beat the disease without the help offered in the treatment facilities. Many of them left treatment and returned to their old behavior in short order. As *Alcoholics Anonymous* describes them, these patients who do not get the program are "constitutionally incapable of being honest with themselves."[31] They cling to the delusion that at some point in the future they will become master of alcohol rather than the other way around. But, I listened to what the counselors and the AA "winners" told me, i.e. once an alcoholic, always an alcoholic. Once we lose control over alcohol, we can never regain control, if we ever controlled it in the first place.

Changing my attitude toward counseling helped immensely in my recovery. I stopped fighting the attempts to get inside my emotional life and let them in. Only then did I begin to feel better. I learned that I could not help my feelings and therefore should not feel guilty about how I felt. I learned that identifying how I felt and talking about it did not mean I was weak; in fact, I believe it takes a stronger person to admit to feelings than to disguise and deny them. Once I realized that I had a great deal of resentment, fear, self-pity and envy bottled up inside me, I took my counselors' suggestions about actions I could take to bring them out and almost immediately, I started to get better. When I commenced from in-patient treatment several years ago, I had the strong feeling that the compulsion to drink had left me. I somehow felt that this time, I might make it without drinking. So far, that has been the case.

Work the 12 Steps

In my drinking days, I became skeptical about many things, such as AA and their steps, traditions, and mottos by which to live. I thought of all of that as mystical nonsense, but this time around, I have come to believe that working the 12 steps, reading the literature, confiding in a sponsor and applying the mottos to my life, has taught me to live without the negative emotions I carried around with me everywhere, while drinking. I learned to "live life on life's terms," rather than on alcohol's terms. By continuing to do these things over the course of years, I have remained free of the compulsion to drink and without the compulsion, not drinking is easy. With the compulsion, not drinking is the hardest thing in the world for an alcoholic.

Though I had read the steps and heard others read them many times at AA meetings, I really did not understand them until I got serious about changing my life. A number of AA members have proposed suggestions for the best ways to work the steps, but I learned that everyone has his/her unique way of doing them and for someone else to interfere may endanger sobriety. Suffice it to say, getting honest with oneself is the most important step. Without successfully working the first step, the others almost always fail to produce the serenity and peace that displace the compulsion to drink in recovering alcoholics. After internalizing the idea that I could never drink safely again, the program became easier for me. If I could not drink safely again, I had to figure out how to live without alcohol. Around this initial stage of recovery, I started to see how getting honest with myself led me to see things differently than before and that honesty allowed me to see how much alcohol had consumed most of my prior life. Before this stark look at myself, I managed to convince myself that I controlled my drinking and that alcohol amused me. But in my newfound honesty, I saw how alcohol absorbed me into a trap. I had become unable to function well without it. I could not imagine enjoying myself socially if I could not drink alcohol.

Having realized that I cannot drink safely again, I had an empty feeling, like my life had ended. But as time went on, I realized that I could do almost anything I set my mind to now that I no longer allowed drinking to consume so much time and effort. Also, since I did not become immobilized by alcohol every day, I had time to devote to whatever else I wanted to do. Because I wanted to get better and to relieve the compulsion to drink, I spent some time consciously thinking about working the 12 steps of recovery and then actually doing the work. Because the steps revolve strongly around a spiritual program, I learned that I could "work" Steps 2, 3, 5, 6, 7, 10, and 11, in some measure every day by praying. I formed simple prayers, largely using the wording included in the steps themselves, such as, "God, please remove my character defects; help me to be the best person I can be," and "Help me to know your will for me and give me the strength and courage to carry it out." Mouthing the words does not constitute praying; sincerely thinking them in a communicative manner to the God of my understanding does.

I do not intend to go into detail about how I worked and continue to work the steps. I strongly suggest that anyone who wants to try to work them (and anyone who sincerely wants to quit drinking but finds doing so difficult falls into this category) should go to an AA meeting and buy a copy of the "Big Book," *Alcoholics Anonymous*, written by the founding members of that brotherhood/sisterhood. I cannot describe the steps or the methods suggested to work them in a manner more likely to produce good results than the original authors did. They paved the way for the rest of us. I learned that I had gotten better about being honest with myself when I read the book and realized that almost everything I read about pertained to me, how I drank, and how I lived while I drank. Now, the sections that describe life without alcohol also directly speak to me. I am one of them and for the first time in a long time, I know I fit in someplace. I also recommend arranging for an AA sponsor to help work the steps, someone who has done them before and who has a substantial period of sobriety, like one or more years.

The steps do not address how to stop drinking; they address how to stay stopped. This particular problem plagues alcoholics more than just stopping. Most of us have stopped for some periods of time, in some cases extended periods of years, but without relieving the compulsion to drink, we will drink again. The compulsion eventually overwhelms us and because we have the disease we have, we will delude ourselves into thinking a sufficient excuse has arisen and we go off to the races again. Some of us never make it back from these sprees. What many of us falsely believe is that extended periods of not drinking entitle us to start over again, to drink "normally." This has never happened with alcoholics; the disease progresses whether or not we drink and starting to drink again after some time off puts us farther down the road to perdition than we were when we stopped.

Help Others

The twelfth step in the recovery process calls for us to help others. While the authors of *Alcoholics Anonymous* seemed to address the need for recovering alcoholics to focus helpful efforts toward alcoholics who have not begun to recover, as a general principle of action, we need to shift the focus in our minds from ourselves to others. I agree that we have an obligation to help other suffering alcoholics, because nobody else stands as great a chance of getting through to them to start down the recovery path than we do. But, some of us have the capability to help other people who are not alcoholics, because of our professions or unique training, and a life spent in service to others fills the bill for us to "get out of ourselves," regardless of whether we help alcoholics or non-alcoholics.

Among the many stories I have heard in the rooms of Alcoholics Anonymous, a common theme emerges that practicing alcoholics think almost exclusively about themselves. Many of us become self-absorbed over an extended period of time, but I know of no exceptions to the rule that to the exclusion of everyone else and everything else in life, we strongly pursue satisfaction to our craving. We obsess over when and where the next drink will come from and once we begin our next drinking episode, we rarely let anything interfere with that process. If we have some reason to go somewhere where we cannot drink alcohol openly, we often take it with us, hide it, and sneak drinks when we believe we do so without detection. We make excuses not go places where we cannot drink openly or have only a slight chance of sneaking it and getting away with it. Without alcohol, we become distressed and approach anti-social behavior. With alcohol, we become depressed and withdrawn anyway, so succeed in isolating ourselves socially from our families and friends over the compulsion to drink alcohol.

In early recovery, alcoholics often find it difficult to reach out to other people. We have lost the touch, so to speak. We have not practiced this skill in the recent (and maybe distant) past. Groups like Alcoholics Anonymous offer an immediate solution to this problem. Just by attending meetings, we can help other people. Every person who shows up at an AA meeting helps someone else, in my opinion. The newcomer demonstrates to the old-timers that alcohol still destroys lives. After substantial periods of sobriety, some alcoholics begin to drift toward the thought processes that we have come to refer to in AA as "stinking thinking." We may get complacent and thoughts begin to appear in the line of, maybe I can drink a little bit now that I haven't had a drink in a long time. Maybe

I can control my drinking now. But, millions of us have learned the hard way that once we become an alcoholic, we will always be an alcoholic. We cannot go backward.

The mid-timers in AA and other such support groups help everyone else present, as well. Newcomers relate better to people who have a little more sobriety than they have than they do members of the 15 to 20 or more years of sobriety group. Seeing that these midtermers have sobriety, serenity and happiness that has eluded the recently sober recovering alcoholic encourages the newcomers to keep at it. Good things do result from working the program and staying sober. Old-timers in AA help everyone, including themselves, by showing that alcoholics can recover for extended periods, living healthy, normal and happy lives. The maxim that we often hear first in our encounter with AA, "Keep coming back," applies to all recovering alcoholics. We gain strength and hope from each other, whether we have one day or multiple years of sobriety.

Once newcomers become comfortable with attending AA meetings, they begin to see how they can help other alcoholics, both in the AA rooms and out. The world has millions of practicing alcoholics, many of whom actually want to quit drinking and straighten out their lives, but do not know what to do. By remaining sober and thereby gaining health and sanity in our behavior, we set an example that others will want to emulate. Eventually, heavy drinking wears people down and they will arrive at turning points in their lives. Either we quit drinking or go on to miserable death, unless we end up in prison or in an insane asylum. Some do not quit and among these unfortunates, most end up dying before they normally would, going to prison or finding themselves committed to an insane asylum. For those who choose the other path, freedom from obsession and a new life result. Sharing this newfound freedom with others becomes the ticket to continued sobriety and increased happiness. Given that practicing alcoholics who have not decided to quit drinking will usually not recover until they decide to turn their lives around, we do not actively pursue them. By setting an example, those who want what we have will come to us seeking help. We should always help those who ask for it.

We often learn through working the 12 steps or recovery that some people who do not have the disease of alcoholism have other problems with which we can help. We have survived a terrible disease that has taken many of us close to death. When we recover, we realize how blessed we have been. Therefore, when other people who obviously lack serenity come into our lives, we practice acceptance and patience with them, as the 12 step program teaches us to do. By setting an example for them, we hope to help them, just like we hope to help suffering alcoholics turn their lives around. A number of recovering alcoholics have related stories about non-alcoholics who have confronted the recovering alcoholics with statements on the order of, "I wish I felt like you seem to feel." We radiate serenity and self-esteem, once we move into recovery. We have done something that few people manage without difficulty. Others want to share those feelings.

129

The most obvious place to start looking for people to help, aside from AA or other such support groups, is within our families. After long-term alcohol abuse by one of its members, rarely does a family emerge unscathed. By demonstrating that we have become willing to change and by taking measures to do so, we help our spouses, children, parents, etc. By living according to the spiritual principles of the recovery program, we set another positive example for all around us. Though it takes time for the healing process to run through a family, that process occurs in nearly all cases in which a recovering alcoholic is involved. Our drunken behavior has created numerous problems in our spouses and children that cannot get resolved overnight. But, the healing process begins almost immediately, and if we continue to work our recovery program, that healing process will continue. Many families grow stronger bonds than they ever had before through weathering the alcoholic storm together.

The recovery process lasts for a lifetime and therefore, the requirement to help others continues for the rest of recovering alcoholics' lives. Especially in the cases of the families of recovering alcoholics, the helping process must continue for the rest of their lives. Some alcoholics who start the recovery process fall prey to the misconception that working the steps is a one time process that guarantees sobriety. After a short period of seeking out and helping others, the misconception that their "ticket punches" now entitle them to slacken off. Even if indulging in this misconception does not immediately lead to drinking again, and in most cases it will, the alcoholic who reverts to self-centered behavior will live miserably. As *Alcoholics Anonymous* points out, selfishness causes the problems that alcoholics typically experience.[32] We must continue to seek out and help other people as long as we live, if we want to live at all happily and soberly.

Some recovering alcoholics who have experienced a "spiritual renewal" as the result of the 12 step program mistakenly believe that they now have the right to impose their newfound spirituality on everyone around them, especially their family members. Not only does this not work, in most cases, it tends to sour relationships already severely tainted through long periods of alcoholic behavior. We should settle for leadership by example instead of a course of action involving converting others through preaching to them. We got sober and changed our lives because of our higher power's help and we should have internalized the message of acceptance of others in all our endeavors. We hear in AA and in counseling that we cannot change anyone but ourselves. This truism leads to the conclusion that our recovery program requires us to accept others as they are or avoid interacting with them. Acceptance of others did not occur to us during our drinking days; we attempted to manipulate everyone around us for our own purposes. Changing this attitude and behavior, necessary for our recovery, takes effort. We do not immediately excel at it, but we keep trying to get better at it. Helping others, then, does not mean trying to change them. We should show them how our lives have changed through our actions and help them with the problems of life, when appropriate, but not with an eye toward making them change. Only they can manage a change in themselves; we can advise them if asked, but we should not preach to them.

Another of the many stories that I commonly hear in AA meetings involves the recognition among recovering alcoholics that many more people knew about our alcoholism than we realized when we drank. We tried hard to hide the facts about how much and how frequently we drank. In many cases, because other people did not mention anything to us about our drinking, we believed that we had successfully fooled those around us about our drinking abuse. Only after we have achieved sobriety for some time do we begin to discover that almost everyone with whom we had daily contact, family members, co-workers, bosses, social associates, etc. knew about our drinking problems and they congratulate us on not drinking, once they know we have entered into recovery. They find it much easier to talk to us about it in sobriety than to confront us with it when we might become belligerent or worse because of alcohol in our systems. However, we recovering alcoholics have an advantage over those who know a practicing alcoholic who needs help and do not have the disease themselves. While we should usually wait for a lucid moment to intervene, sometimes we can save a life or make a big difference in a lot of lives by confronting an alcoholic under the influence. Once we have clearly identified ourselves as recovering alcoholics and demonstrate with our stories that we know what the suffering alcoholics go through, we might make a dent in their armor. Though they may continue for some time to lie to themselves and pursue self-destruction, the dent can get larger over time and sometimes that one seed of doubt about themselves cast by someone who knows alcoholism, can grow into a blooming flower. So long as a practicing alcoholic can say with certainty that intervening persons do not know what they are talking about, little hope exists that the alcoholics will stop drinking long enough to try to evaluate themselves. When people who clearly know what they are talking about make the intervention, then the suffering person cannot hide behind the shield of claiming that other people who are ignorant of how they feel just want to mess with them.

Helping others takes many forms. Helping suffering alcoholics to get dry and to begin a program of recovery represents one way to help. Others take the forms of helping needy people (alcoholic or non-alcoholic) with employment, residences, etc. In any of these cases, recovering alcoholics continue to work their programs and build up credit against falling back into selfishness and therefore, drunkenness, by focusing on doing things for others rather than focusing on themselves. In the cases of newly recovering alcoholics though, nothing should replace the focus on help with not drinking. Jobs, places to live, marriages, other personal relationships, etc. take a back seat to sobriety. None of them are possible for any extended time period without sobriety for alcoholics. Also, though some alcoholics believe otherwise, their recoveries do not depend on having jobs, places to live, personal relationships, etc. A great many alcoholics have none of these things, but recover from the disease. Usually, when well into recovery, alcoholics find that these well-worth-having things come back easily, so long as the alcoholics remain sober. The cycle must then continue, as the newly recovering alcoholics begin to help others, thus strengthening themselves more.

VIII
What To Do If Someone You Know Has This Disease

Get Honest

One of the ironic characteristics of alcoholism lies in how it affects the people close to the alcoholics themselves. Very often, family members, bosses, co-workers, friends, etc. fall into the trap of denial, just as the alcoholic does. I believe that one cause of this phenomena is the acceptance of the myths about alcoholism as a moral character defect, rather than as a treatable disease. In many cases, because spouses, parents, etc. do not know that the alcoholic spouse, child, employee, etc. is sick, they fall into the pattern of denial. Fear of the unknown causes humans to do some strange things when it comes to protecting loved ones and even protecting our own reputations. We do not like for other people to think of us as the wife or husband of an alcoholic. So, we attempt to hide the facts in these cases. Denial takes many forms in the cases of the people close to the alcoholics themselves. Sometimes we joke about the drinking behavior, minimalize the extent to which others drink, rationalize for the alcoholics that they feel stress from the job, etc. But in truth, we do not help the suffering alcoholics of this world by denying the truth. Alcoholics need help and diverting attention away from someone who needs help contributes to the problem.

Another hindrance to families and friends getting involved in alcoholics' recovery takes the form of another misunderstanding. Because the alcoholics involved will almost assuredly deny they have problems with alcohol, the intervener may decide to accept this explanation on the basis that nothing can get done unless the alcoholics themselves acknowledge the disease. If they don't want help, then we can do nothing, sometimes summarizes the thinking of the potential intervener. But, I think it imperative that everyone around suffering alcoholics get honest with themselves as quickly as possible, if they intend to help the alcoholics. Whether the practicing alcoholics themselves ever acknowledge their diseases or not, those who interact with alcoholics surely feel the affects of alcohol abuse. Accepting that people whose lives touch ours suffer from alcoholism helps us understand and plan our actions accordingly. The best thing to do if people we know are alcoholics is to learn as much about the disease as we can and develop strategies for doing something about it.

Once we know that we have alcoholic family members, friends, employees, co-workers, etc., we should do something quickly. The longer we wait, the more difficult the challenge in recovery will become. Though many alcoholics will continue to deny their problems after their initial confrontation, the delusion that they are fooling us completely should disappear. At this point, it becomes likely that the practicing alcoholics will reach a crisis. They cannot stop drinking and they know that someone else knows how much and how often they drink. In extreme efforts to develop a plan to continue drinking and keep it a secret, they often find the efforts fruitless and take the first step toward recovery, admitting they need help to stop drinking.

Depending on our relationships with alcoholics, we may need to become honest with ourselves about ourselves. We may be co-dependents or other role playing agents in these situations and require help ourselves. If someone we love has this disease, we may well suffer from psychological and sociological problems, as well. In these cases, professional help also means return to normalcy and the support groups, like Al Anon and Al Ateen, provide a place to go to talk about this phenomenon for free. Just like alcoholics avoiding going to AA meetings because of the stigma they imagine attaches to doing so, some co-dependents and children of alcoholics refuse to go to Al Anon or Al Ateen because of this imagined stigma. Anyone who would ostracize us because we attempted to get help in these matters should not be considered a friend anyway. Seek help.

Change Your Attitude

I advised alcoholics who want to recover to change their attitudes from self-centered, self-pity indulging, etc. to become grateful for what they have. The same applies to the families and friends of alcoholics. Though alcoholism in a home or in a relationship usually wreaks havoc, to focus on what alcohol has cost us hurts all of our chances to get better. Focus, instead, on what we have for which to give thanks. Most of us have much more to be grateful for than to lament losing due to alcohol. When any of us indulge ourselves in self-pity, we lose the opportunity of the moment to become better people. Getting better from the disease means we need to concentrate on becoming better people.

I know a few members of Al Anon whose alcoholic spouses still drink. These spouses of alcoholics recognize the disease in their husbands and wives, even though the suffering alcoholics themselves do not see it. To seek help through Al Anon does not require that the alcoholics involved have already sought help. In fact, seeking help for ourselves sometimes motivates them to do something for themselves. But more often, by attending Al Anon and Al Ateen meetings, those non-alcoholic victims of alcoholism can find others to help who will in turn help them to get better. Those of us who have weathered the storm of alcoholism, either as a recovering alcoholic or co-dependent, have unique opportunities to help those still struggling with the disease and its affects. Few things in life reward us as much as knowing that our efforts have made someone else's life better. By caring and showing others that we care, we can make a huge difference in solving these problems. I recommend that we all reach out to those who need help as a means of helping ourselves.

Along with the shift in focus from ourselves, we should try to accept those things in life over which we have no control, change those things needing changes, and seek help from our higher power to know what we have control over and what we don't. These sentiments from the Serenity Prayer that many AA groups incorporate into their meetings, sum up the recovery program for both alcoholics and others affected by the disease.[33] Sometimes, because practicing alcoholics abuse us so much, those of us who are alcoholism's non-alcoholic victims (second hand drinking, so to speak) become bitter and mean in our dealings with other people. Like alcoholics, we sometimes mistakenly believe that most people drink and most of our lots in life are driven by alcohol. Changing those attitudes for non-alcoholic victims of alcoholics can be difficult, but not impossible. By reaching out, we will find that many others have gone through what we have and survived. We also find out that by changing their attitudes to more positive ones, they have made their lives take a turn for the better. I suggest spending time with people with positive attitudes rather than negative attitudes. Pay attention to the silver linings around dark clouds. Even our worst days have some positive aspect to them and the most terrible day will look better tomorrow, for most of us.

One of the most important attitude changes comes with becoming aware that alcoholism is a disease and that the alcoholics in our lives do not intentionally hurt us. The abusive words or deeds come from the alcohol, not the person. In the majority of alcoholics, once alcohol leaves their lives through recovery, they become caring, understanding human beings. Knowing that these sick people can change and that our lives, in turn, can get better can lead us to an understanding and acceptance. We do not treat cancer victims or victims of other diseases with contempt because we know the sick people cannot help having the disease. Alcoholism, though, because it triggers aggressive and abusive behavior in many alcoholics, is somewhat different, though terminally ill patients with other diseases often withdraw emotionally from their loved ones and become abusive and mean.

We should not continue to place ourselves in the positions to get hurt, physically or emotionally. But, I suggest that we realize that if the alcoholics in our lives do recover, then we can usually safely renew our relationships with them and build stronger bonds than we had before the disease began to ravage everyone affected. If we love the suffering alcoholics for the persons they were before the disease took over their lives, then it would seem worth the effort to weather the alcoholic storm in order to renew wonderful relationships

In cases in which the alcoholic has not become abusive, we can seek help for ourselves, stay connected at some level with the alcoholics and hope that they seek help sooner rather than later in the progression of their disease. Like cancer victims, encouraging alcoholics to seek help without becoming overbearing about it, sometimes moves the recovery process along more quickly. But, as many alcoholics remain in denial for long periods of time, non-alcoholic victims of alcoholism should not put off their recovery until the alcoholics come to their senses. For all concerned, the sooner we get help, the better. Sometimes, leaving AA literature around where our alcoholic family members might find it helps them. If they read it and begin to question their own lives, then they may convince themselves that they need help. Seldom do they seek help when badgered by people who do not have the experiences that practicing alcoholics have.

Seek Counseling

For non-alcoholic victims of alcoholism, professional counseling takes on as much importance as it does for alcoholics. Many co-dependents and children of alcoholics mistakenly believe that they do not have emotional and psychological problems, but that the entire set of problems in their lives will disappear when their alcoholic family member recovers or leaves their lives. Unfortunately, this belief has proven false in every recorded case. In many cases, alcoholics move into recovery, but their family members do not and the alcoholics get better, physically, emotionally, and psychologically, while their family members do not get better. I know some marriages that have broken up in such cases. The alcoholics, following the advice of counselors and AA, began to get better, at varying paces, but their family members did not understand their own needs for help and large rifts appeared in their relationships. Sometimes, spouses of recovering alcoholics begin to wish their alcoholic spouses would start drinking again, so things would revert to the status quo.

Counseling for non-alcoholic victims of alcoholism varies, but often the individual counseling precedes any family counseling that is required. The Al –Anon program that mirrors AA in providing support for non-alcoholic victims of alcoholism works in the same way that AA works for alcoholics. It provides a support group of people who have had similar experiences as the newcomer, but more importantly, it suggests a way to change lives in a positive way. Using the same 12 step program as that used in AA, the non-alcoholic victims of alcoholism learn to "live life on life's terms." They learn to accept the difficulties of life without resorting to self-destructive behavior other than drinking alcohol.

In many cases, counselors can identify the common cycle that emerges in many alcoholic families; many children of alcoholics marry alcoholics in adulthood without knowing that either their parents or their spouses are alcoholics. The non-alcoholic spouses know the ropes, so to speak, in dealing with alcoholic family members and take on similar roles for the spouses as they performed for their parents. In the worst cases, co-dependents go through several failed marriages with alcoholics, because they cannot identify the problem as alcoholism. Much like the denial that alcoholics go through, co-dependents often go into denial, blaming other people, places and things for the troubles in their families' lives, when the real cause, alcoholism, plainly shows itself to outsiders looking in.

I believe that co-dependents and children of alcoholics get trapped into these depths of denial because of mistakenly accepting the myth of moral choice making on the parts of the alcoholics in their lives. Embarrassment over having a loving relationship with a "morally degenerate" person causes them to seek other explanations and thus, deflect the moral responsibility onto someone or something else. The typical pattern of lying to employers, to extended family members and friends about the alcoholics' behavior, the gradual social isolation and other such common patterns of behavior among the families of alcoholics seems to stem from fear of what others will think of them. If most people accepted alcoholism as a disease, instead of as a moral deficiency, family members might seek help earlier and more often, rather than shrinking into denial along with their alcoholic family member. Like alcoholics, the co-dependents often respond more positively to other co-dependents or children of alcoholics who have a first hand knowledge and experience of what they have gone through, than to counselors. However, like alcoholics, non-alcoholic family members need counseling in addition to the support of Al-Anon and other groups of recovering co-dependents. Admitting the need for help and seeking help will start the non-alcoholic family members moving toward a more rewarding life than they have experienced before.

Work the 12 Steps

During the drinking careers of alcoholics their families unintentionally usually enter into the same types of behavior that characterizes the alcoholics themselves. The non-alcoholic family members move into denial, become dishonest in addressing the behavior of their alcoholic family members, socially withdraw in attempting to keep the alcoholic behavior a secret, hurt other people (sometimes intentionally and sometimes unintentionally) through words and deeds, and generally feel trapped in a world about which they know something has gone wrong, but cannot identify the real causes. As a result, the non-alcoholic members of alcoholics have become self-centered, deeply immersed in self-pity and prone to fear and resentments, the same problems that plague their alcoholic family members. To counter these negative feelings and positively change the lives of non-alcoholic victims of alcoholism, the 12 step program of recovery works as well with co-dependents and children of alcoholics as it does with alcoholics.

People not intimately familiar with the 12 step recovery program may think this advice curious, since they mistakenly believe that the authors of the program intended to get alcoholics to quit drinking through its suggestions. However, the 12 step program actually involves a formula for good living. Alcoholics face the dual problem of quitting drinking and then staying sober. Solving the first part of this dual problem involves removing alcohol from the alcoholics' lives, usually accomplished in a medical environment. The second part of the problem presents a more difficult challenge for alcoholics and medical professionals. Even after extended time periods without alcohol, alcoholics not in recovery experience a fierce compulsion to drink. The 12 step program provides a guide for changing our lives in such ways that the compulsion to drink leaves us. When we have that compulsion, we will eventually drink again, whether the next day, week, month or year. Without the compulsion, we may live and die soberly, an impossibility without a recovery program

In the 12 steps, the word "alcohol" appears only once, in the first step and there it refers to admitting our powerlessness over alcohol, not how to stop drinking. By changing the way we live and feel about life, we overcome the compulsion to drink. Interestingly, support groups for people with other forms of addictive diseases, like drug addiction, overeating, gambling, etc. have adopted the same 12 step process to recover from these addictive diseases. Similarly, non-alcoholic victims of alcoholism need to change their behaviors and feelings (attitudes) in order to fully recover normalcy in their lives.

Non-alcoholic victims of alcoholism also have to get honest with themselves, just as recovering alcoholics must. Non-alcoholic victims must admit that their loved ones have a serious, but controllable disease and that they have denied this to themselves for a long time. Often, the spouses, children and other loved ones of alcoholics blame themselves for their alcoholic loved ones' drinking and behavior. But, though alcoholics often blame their family members, the disease, and nothing else, causes this alcoholic drinking and negative behavior associated with drunkenness. Part of getting honest with ourselves as non-alcoholic victims of alcoholism involves realizing and accepting that we have not caused the alcoholics in our lives to drink. The other part involves realizing that we need help and that our behavior has hurt other people, too. Each of the 12 steps has meaning for us, as well. We should develop a spiritual program of living, make a serious introspective look into ourselves to assess where we need improvement, identify who we have hurt in our lives, make amends to those where appropriate and continue this process every day thereafter.

By concentrating on this lifestyle based on spiritual principles, non-alcoholic victims of the alcoholic disease begin to feel better, begin to accept life's situations over which they have no control and develop a focus on helping others rather than on pitying themselves. Like recovering alcoholics, recovering non-alcoholic victims of alcoholism begin to feel better almost immediately. Also, they feel a sense of hope that had eluded them while deluding themselves. Like recovering alcoholics, they feel "a new peace and a new freedom."[34] If the recovering non-alcoholic victims of alcoholism and the alcoholics in their lives work this 12 step program together, they often form a much stronger emotional bond than they ever had before. But, if they cannot work the program together, either or both should work it alone, with the support of AA or Al-Anon, because the sooner everyone recovers, the better. Waiting does not make sense for anyone.

Helping Others

As recovering alcoholics find meaning in their lives by helping other alcoholics to recover from their diseases, non-alcoholic victims of alcoholism can find similar rewards by helping other people. As with alcoholics, who get better by helping anyone in need of help not just helping alcoholics to recover, non-alcoholic victims can get better by helping anyone in need of any help. But, non-alcoholic victims of alcoholism often find it difficult to identify needy people when initially working the 12 step program. In these cases, I recommend going to Al-Anon to find others who have had similar experiences with alcoholic family members to help. Anyone who has weathered the storm of living in close proximity to practicing alcoholics has multiple opportunities in the communities to help others still going through the storm.

As with practicing alcoholics, non-alcoholic victims of alcoholism who have not come to grips with their denial, delusional behavior, dishonesty, resentments, and self-pity will most likely relate best to someone who has had similar experiences than to anyone else, including professional counselors. The propensity to believe that nobody else has felt like they feel or experienced the same things they have experienced can usually only be cracked by listening to people, who through relating their stories, clearly know about what they speak. If we can convince the suffering victim that we've traveled the same road, discovered a solution and altered our lives for the better, then the victims may want what we have. To start this way, usually leads to another successful recovery for non-alcoholic victims of alcoholism.

The 12 step program provides a promising guide for life for everyone, including people not suffering from addictive diseases. For alcoholics, non-alcoholic victims of alcoholism, and victims of other addictions, it offers the most reliable source of hope among all other potential solutions. Getting out of ourselves and genuinely caring about helping others becomes the source of our greatest satisfaction in life. Happiness comes as a bi-product of doing something for someone else, not as a result of seeking happiness. Those of us who have gone to the depths of despair that alcoholism can lead to and then recovered, have a bond with each other that many people never acquire in their lives. We believe that God has blessed us by giving us the ability to give to others the gift of recovery we have received.

IX
Conclusion

This book does not offer a comprehensive plan of recovery from alcoholism or from the suffering that results from loving and living with an alcoholic. Anyone who wants to recover from alcoholism should get, read and practice the suggestions laid out in *Alcoholics Anonymous* or one of the other books about recovery from addictive diseases that uses the 12 step program. I have related my experiences with the disease, its consequences and my recovery so that people who read this and may become motivated to change their lives will have some idea of where to start and then what to do. But, I also intended to identify some of the myths that abound concerning alcoholism in particular, and addictive diseases in general, in hopes that more people will understand the nature of this deadly disease and those afflicted with it directly and indirectly. Most importantly, I hope to raise awareness of the ethical issues involved in perpetuation of belief in these myths. Among all the theories of normative ethics proposed to explain moral judgments, none would allow blaming and punishing people whose actions have not resulted from a rational choice of free will, but rather from foggy or non-existent judgment, temporary insanity or both. Our laws clearly reflect widespread belief in these myths of freedom of choice, both in regard to choosing to drink on the parts of alcoholics and choosing behavior while under the influence of alcohol. Neither of these judgments holds up in light of medical research results or the experiences of recovering alcoholics. I hope that my rather unique position as the adult child of an alcoholic, an alcoholic (now gratefully in recover) and a professor of ethics can help shed light on these issues. I hope mostly that through education, understanding and desire for fairness and betterment of society, we will make strong strides toward solving the variety of problems alcoholism causes through understanding its true nature, a debilitating, potentially deadly disease that can be arrested. There is a solution and there is hope.

Endnotes

1. *Alcoholics Anonymous: The Story of How Many Thousands of Men and Women Have Recovered from Alcoholism*, Fourth Edition, Alcoholics Anonymous World Services, Inc., 2001, p. 59 (hereafter sited as A.A.).

2. "One Day at a Time" is often read at Alcoholics Anonymous meetings. The original source is unknown.

3. A.A., pp. xxvii-xxxii.

4. A.A., p. xxx.

5. A.A., p. 21.

6. Cole, K.C., "Calculated Risks," in *The Longwood Reader*, Edward A. Damron and Michael Finnegan, Pearson Education, Inc., p. 241.

7. A.A., p. 21.

8. Education segment of treatment for alcoholism.

9. A.A., pp. xxviii-xxix.

10. A.A., p. 21.

11. A.A., pp. 58-59.

12. A.A., p. 30.

13. Kant, Immanuel, *The Foundations of the Metaphysics of Morals,* in *Introduction to Philosophy: Classical and Contemporary Reading,* Louis P. Pojman, Oxford University Press, New York, 2004, pp. 587-598.

14. A.A. p. 30.

15. Woititz, Janet, *The Adult Children of Alcoholics,* Health Communications, Inc., Deerfield Beach, FL, 1983.

16. A.A., p. 82.

17. A.A., p. 21.

18. A.A., p. 23.

19. A.A., p. 62.

20. A.A., p. 84.

21. A.A., p. xxiii.

22. A.A., p. 33.

23. A.A., p. xxix.

24. A.A., p. 73.

25. A.A., p. 82.

26. A.A., p.57.

27. A.A., p. 34.

28. A.A., p. 62.

29. A.A., p. 62.

30. A.A., p. 59.

31. A.A., p. 58.

32. A.A., p. 62.

33. "The Serenity Prayer" is often read at AA meetings.

34. A.A., p. 83.

About the Author

James McDonough is uniquely qualified to write about the topics of alcoholism and the Ethical implications thereof as a recovering alcoholic and Adjunct Professor of Philosophy, specializing in teaching Ethics. Having personally experienced the ravages of alcoholism on himself and his family, he decided to share his experiences in the hope that other alcoholics and addictive people and their families might find hope in recovery as well. Also, having suffered the penalties and other negative consequences of the misunderstandings and myths associated with alcoholism and addictive diseases, he hoped to help non-alcoholic and non-addictive people to understand addiction as a disease caused by chemical imbalances and the cycle of recovery from addictions, so that we might correct the unwarranted moral judgments that many people make about alcoholics and addicts based on these misunderstandings and myths.

www.ingramcontent.com/pod-product-compliance
Lightning Source LLC
Chambersburg PA
CBHW061257280526
45784CB00002B/788